The Autism Couple's Workbook

The Autism Couple's Workbook, Second Edition

MAXINE ASTON

Foreword by
TONY ATTWOOD

Illustrated by
WILLIAM ASTON and ANTONY CORBETT

Jessica Kingsley Publishers
London and Philadelphia

First published in Great Britain in 2009 by Jessica Kingsley Publishers
An Hachette Company

This edition published in Great Britain in 2021 by Jessica Kingsley Publishers
An Hachette Company

2

Copyright © Maxine Aston 2009, 2021
Foreword copyright © Tony Attwood 2021
Illustrations copyright © William Aston and Antony Corbett 2021

A CIP catalogue record for this title is available from the British Library and the Library of Congress

978 1 78592 891 8
978 1 78592 892 5

Printed and bound by CPI Group (UK) Ltd, Croydon, CR0 4YY

Jessica Kingsley Publishers' policy is to use papers that are natural, renewable and recyclable
products and made from wood grown in sustainable forests. The logging and manufacturing
processes are expected to conform to the environmental regulations of the country of origin.

Jessica Kingsley Publishers
73 Collier Street
London N1 9BE, UK

www.jkp.com

For R

Difference can only feel threatening if it exists in the absence of acceptance and understanding.

Maxine Aston (2008)

Contents

Foreword

Maxine's original workbook was published in 2009, and in the intervening years she has continued to explore relationships where one or both partners have the characteristics of autism. I have eagerly anticipated this revised and expanded edition, looking forward to learning about Maxine's recent discoveries based on her extensive experience of counselling couples, her conversations with colleagues and her reviews of relevant research.

Since 2013 we have new diagnostic criteria for autism in the fifth edition of the *Diagnostic and Statistical manual of Mental Disorders (DSM5)*. Criterion A3 specifically refers to 'deficits in developing, maintaining, and understanding relationships' as a core characteristic of autism, and it is this characteristic that is a central component of relationship counselling. The new DSM dispenses with the term Asperger's syndrome, replacing it with Autism Spectrum Disorder, hence the title of the revised workbook being updated to *The Autism Couple's Workbook, Second Edition.*

There are many positive attributes of autism that are appealing to a prospective partner. The person can be extraordinarily attentive, knowledgeable, creative, kind, endearingly immature, physically attractive, quiet, and inexperienced in romantic relationships. There can be compassion for their limited social abilities and their having been the victim of teasing and bullying at school and work. The potential autistic partner is often appreciated for being predictable, honest, and confident in their opinions, with shared interests and perhaps an admired career. They may have similar characteristics to one of the parents of the neurotypical partner, such that this partner is already fluent in the language and culture of autism. In the early stages of the relationship, the neurotypical partner may not be aware of their autistic partner's history or profile of abilities, anticipating instead a conventional relationship, which, if needed, would benefit from conventional relationship counselling.

Clinical experience and research have identified that both autistic males and females may develop a compensatory mechanism of camouflaging social and inter-personal difficulties in the early, romantic stage of the relationship. They may have acquired what appears to be expertise in being a romantic partner from television or films which, initially and temporarily, have provided a script, a role that can be imitated, and a superficial understanding of the rules of the dating game. This ability to camouflage autism and use scripts and roles can also be used successfully at work and in public, the autistic adult becoming a 'chameleon'. Only their partner knows who is behind the mask, as the true self is gradually revealed in the privacy of home.

For their part, the autistic person may fall in love with someone who has exceptional social understanding and empathy for their difficulties, understanding their confusion in social situations and the degree of their exhaustion from socializing. The autistic adult needs and seeks someone who can be a 'translator' of the autistic perspective to friends and family and is a social mentor who does not criticise their partner for being social naivete or clumsiness. The neurotypical partner takes on the role of 'executive secretary' to help with organizational problems, and is able to help their partner cope with change and the unexpected; they continue many of the social and emotional support functions previously provided by a parent.

After several years of living together, the couple may find that the relationship may not be evolving as they originally expected. There may be a sense of grieving for the seemingly elusive conventional relationship once hoped for. For the neurotypical partner, characteristics that were endearing at the start of the relationship subsequently becomes a problem and a source of conflict. The initial optimism that their partner will gradually change and become more emotionally mature and socially skilled can dissolve into despair; social skills appear to be static due to limited motivation to be more sociable, or require constant prompting. The autistic person needs periods of social isolation at home to recover from the social aspects of work, and joint social contact with friends and family can slowly diminish. Gradually, the neurotypical partner reluctantly agrees to reduce the frequency and duration of social contact for the sake of their partner, and slowly absorbs the characteristics of autism into their own personality and lifestyle. A significant problem for the neurotypical partner is a sense of loneliness within the relationship. In contrast, the autistic partner can be content with their own company for long periods of time – alone, but not lonely. Conversations from the point of view of the neurotypical partner can be superficial, but from the perspective of the autistic partner, are satisfying, and primarily an exchange of information, rather than an enjoyment of each other's company, experiences, and shared opinions.

Generally, there is an expectation in an intimate relationship of regular expressions of love, affection and emotional support. What may be missing in the autistic/neurotypical relationship are those daily words and gestures of affection, emotional support and reassurance, which can be a contributory factor to low self-esteem and clinical depression. Due to having autism, the autistic partner may not be able to read and know how to respond to subtle non-verbal communication, and can feel that whatever they say or do is not enough to make their partner feel happy. They unintentionally keep getting it wrong and feel excessively criticized and rejected. They may begin to believe that sometimes it is wiser to do or say nothing.

The ability to read subtle, non-verbal communication and contextual cues to determine what someone is thinking and feeling, Theory of Mind, can be impaired for autistic children and adults. My observation when counselling couples where one partner has the characteristics of autism, is that the neurotypical partner can have an impaired Theory of an Autistic Mind. That is, they have difficulty perceiving or determining what the autistic person is thinking and feeling by reading their facial expression and body language; this is because autistic adults often have a limited 'vocabulary' of facial expressions, gestures, and prosody. Another characteristic of autism is alexithymia, that is, having considerable difficulty converting thoughts and emotions into conversational speech, which inhibits the disclosure of thoughts and feelings in a conversation. Thus, there is a breakdown in communicating and understanding each other's thoughts and feelings.

The dynamics and stress within the relationship will inevitably change with the arrival of children, presenting new responsibilities and sources of conflict, such as different parenting styles. The relationship may reach breaking point. The autistic partner will have less access to their stress management strategies, such as solitude or their special interest, which is a source of pleasure, relaxation, and an effective thought blocker. The relationship could be deteriorating, but both partners can be unaware of what to do to support and repair the relationship.

This revised workbook will provide insight into the perspectives of each partner, presenting practical advice and constructive activities to enable mutual understanding and to repair and strengthen the relationship. The suggestions are simple and effective. If the reader is in such a relationship, and unable to benefit from relationship counselling with a specialist who is experienced in counselling someone who has autism, or is reluctant to seek professional help, then this workbook is an excellent starting point. Relationship counsellors will also benefit from the explanations and activities, as their client base will undoubtedly include couples where one or both partners have the characteristics associated with autism..

Professor Tony Attwood, author of
The Complete Guide to Asperger's Syndrome

Acknowledgements

A huge thanks to all the couples and individuals who have offered their feedback on many of the strategies described in this book. Without you, this book would not have been possible. This book is written for you.

Thank you, Professor Tony Attwood – you were the first to encourage me in my research and have over the years continued to offer support, encouragement and advice.

Thank you to Shenny and Mark for sharing a piece of your lives to be included in this book.

A very special thank you to my daughter Zoe (my rock) for taking the time to read through the manuscript and offer freely her valuable opinions and thoughts.

Another very special thank you to my son William, for his advice, talent and patience in the choice and drawing of the sketches for this book.

A very big thank you to Rafael. You have encouraged me throughout the writing of this second edition and have been an endless source of inspiration and support.

I am forever grateful to Peter for helping me to make the first edition of this book possible; no amount of words can express my appreciation.

Thank you, Antony Corbett, for the time and talent in the drawing of the sketches used in the first edition of this book.

Thank you, Jason Thompson, for both support and the information given on alexithymia.

A very big thank you to my beautiful children Zoe, Zara and William and my two wonderful sons-in-law Neil and Dan, and my four truly amazing grandchildren Emily, James, Theo and little Bethany. Thank you for being a constant source of encouragement, support, inspiration and motivation.

Terminology

For ease of use I will refer to the person affected by an autistic spectrum condition as the 'AS partner' and the person not affected by autism – neurotypical – as the 'NT partner'.

I do not use the term disorder; I use instead condition – hence an autism spectrum disorder (ASD) will be referred to as an autistic spectrum condition (ASC).

I will, at times, refer to the couple when one partner is affected by autism and one partner is classed as neurotypical as a neurodiverse couple.

I would also like to mention that this workbook is relevant to all couples, whether they be heterosexual, gay, lesbian, transgendered or transsexual. If one partner has mild autism then the problems that are presented in the relationship will be of a similar nature.

Using This Book

In this book, you will find blank worksheets for you to fill in with your partner (or family members or a therapist). You can either write on these worksheets directly or, if you prefer, you could copy them out.

Introduction

Making difference work

I have worked as a therapist with couples and families where one or more members are on the autistic spectrum for over 20 years. In that time, I have developed strategies that have benefited both the person affected by autism and all their family members.

Living in a family where at least one member is affected by autism can have an impact on all the family members; all will be affected in some way, but not necessarily in the same way. Living with autism is quite different from living with any other disability. It is invisible, there are no apparent physical signs; in most cases, it would appear that the AS family member is doing fine and coping. This appearance of being okay can cause expectations, particularly within communication and social interaction – expectations the AS partner may find difficulty in attaining.

Autism will affect some of the fundamental ingredients required for relationships either to form or to be maintained. Sometimes, relationships may struggle on for years in the belief that things will get better with time. Yet, in an intimate relationship, for example, neither individual is aware of what is causing the problems and persistent misunderstandings. This can wear down the mental and physical health of both and affect their self-esteem and confidence.

Autism can affect a person's ability to automatically empathize emotionally and communicate both verbally and non-verbally. It can affect the ability to express emotions and perceive the emotions of those around them. Most of my work as a therapist has focused on this aspect, in an endeavour to help my clients to find a different way to communicate so that they might understand and work together for the future of their relationship. It is often the obvious that needs addressing – the bringing together of two very different worlds – in order that both might understand and appreciate how these two worlds can be incorporated into a life together.

This book looks to provide a working basis for couples, either on their own or in conjunction with a therapist, to learn new strategies and ideas that will benefit their relationship together and as a family. Many of the ideas in this book come from years of research and years of counselling experience with hundreds of couples and families affected by autism. I do not advocate or propose a specific theory or model for working with couples and families as I believe that all people are different and each person needs to be treated as a unique case. However, there are some fundamental areas that become problematic in an autistic relationship.

Not all the strategies proffered here will apply in every situation. It will be through trial and error that a couple discovers each other, discovers what works for them and how their quality of life and self-esteem might be improved.

Chapter 1

UNDERSTANDING THE DIFFERENCE

T HE majority of couples that come to see me have been struggling to maintain their relationship and make things work for some time. Often, they both feel exhausted, feel their resources are running out and that, despite their individual efforts, the same things keep going wrong, time and time again. Sometimes there is mention of how things used to be in the beginning, how when they first met it was a much happier time, not fraught with so many of the difficulties they now face. The neurotypical (NT) partner will often present as feeling drained and no longer having the energy to make things work. The AS partner may feel constantly under attack as though whatever they do it will never make the NT partner happy.

The different species concept

The NT partner and the AS partner are very different and could be described as different species, neither superior nor inferior, just different. In order to understand this, let us think about the animal kingdom. In the animal kingdom, there are lots of different species. Some are similar but the majority can be easily identified. Each individual species sticks together; they mate together and, for some, spend their lives together. They eat the same food and enjoy the same environment.

Although humans are a species in themselves, there are derivatives, or sociological species, unconnected to variations in physical appearance, within that human species. We are biologically the same, yet we are not necessarily psychologically, sociologically or emotionally the same.

Sometimes two people meet, think they have found a partner who is in tune with them, feel happier than they have for some time and enjoy the new partner's company intensely. Later, this seems to wane for them as differences that were somewhat overlooked in the initial euphoria begin to surface.

Let's imagine an eagle (male) meets a zebra (female). Both are entranced by the uniqueness of each other and they fall in love. They are blissfully happy until one day Eagle flies off into the sky with a view to finding Zebra something really nice to eat. Eagle hunts all day until a hare is caught and, with much effort, flies back with his catch all the way to Zebra's front door.

'Surprise! Surprise!' says Eagle, really excited. 'Look what I have caught for you to eat!'

Zebra is shocked as the dead hare is espied and says, 'But I do not eat meat!' Eagle is mortified and feels rejected; all that effort given little or no recognition; the risk to life and limb to bring such a gift now spurned. At this point, the whole relationship changes as Eagle and Zebra recognize that, although they might share the same environment, might enjoy mutual aspects of that environment, they do not share a need for the same food. Zebra is a herd animal and finds it lonely in Eagle's remote world. Eagle loves Zebra and wants the best for Zebra. Eagle provides everything except that which Zebra really wants or needs – her emotional and social food. Zebra will compromise and try to fit into Eagle's world.

Zebra needs Eagle to be close, attentive and loving, while Eagle needs to rationalize, calculate and be a provider. Zebra thrives on vegetation. Eagle is a meat eater and does not understand why Zebra rejects that which Eagle worked so hard to provide. The result is that Zebra slowly begins to deteriorate from lack of the food she needs to survive and the herding instinct of her own species. This leaves Eagle feeling very hurt. Whatever he does, it does not seem to make Zebra happy and he feels unappreciated for all his efforts.

Different needs

Although human beings are a single species, within that species exist variations that are not as obviously different physically as Eagle and Zebra, but nonetheless exhibit the selfsame emotional and logical disparity. The NT partner and the AS partner think in very different ways. Both need a very different type of food and, for many, a very different environment too. The AS partners need their food to be logical and practical, as their thought processing is quite linear and focused, lending them to being systematic rather than empathic. Most AS partners enjoy being a couple, but what they require from their partner emotionally is often minimal, and when they fail to make their NT partner happy, they can become quite distressed.

The NT partner's needs are quite different. They require their food to be emotional, even idiosyncratic, as their thought processing may be romantic and idealistic, lending them to be adaptable rather than fixed. Most NT partners thrive on the emotional reflection their partner gives them. However, the absence of this reflection will leave them feeling deprived. Unaware that their partner is being deprived of something they are unable to offer, the AS partner experiences a sense of unhappiness as their partner appears not to be as content as they are within the relationship. Neither knows how to change this. They may decide it must be something they are doing wrong, or sometimes, even worse, they decide it is the other's fault and attempt to make them feel guilty.

Becoming aware of or recognizing their differences, particularly where autism exists within a relationship, can be a watershed for change. Until this point, the NT partner and the AS partner were probably unaware of their differences, unaware of their different needs, and sought – potentially detrimentally – to compromise. The NT partner, being more empathic, will have recognized that the AS partner often prefers to be in a solitary environment. The NT partner will come to know that the AS partner cannot feed her, know that she cannot live off the AS partner's food alone, but will stand by the AS partner, believing there is a future together, believing that things can change.

It is likely to be the NT partner who will spend most of the time trying to live in the AS partner's environment, as the AS partner does not have the necessary skills to live in the NT partner's world. The longer the NT partner is outside their environment, deprived of the food they need, the more likely the NT partner will start to lose their identity and become more like the AS partner. The NT partner needs to take care and not let this happen, trying to ensure their needs are met.

As long as neither depends on the other for their food and as long as they make time to be in their respective environments, it is totally possible for the NT partner and the AS partner to enjoy a life together. If both have enough love, commitment and respect for each other within the relationship, then all things are possible. This workbook provides some strategies to help make that possible. There will always be difficulties and struggles when living with another equal but different species, which this book won't change. However, with understanding and acceptance of those differences, allied with a determination by both people to have that life together, improvements in their situation will follow.

A different way of thought processing

In order to be able to understand and accept the differences that exist, a couple will need to understand what it is that makes them think differently, express themselves differently and, in some cases, appear to love each other differently. To explain this, I use the example of research quoted by Rita Carter, author of the excellent book *Mapping the Mind* (1998). I have already written about this research in my book *Aspergers in Love* (Aston 2003b). Since then, I have adapted this explanation in a way that makes sense to my clients and helps them to understand both themselves and their partner.

Carter discusses an experiment (Fletcher *et al.* 1995) that used positron emission tomography (PET), a brain-scanning technique that produces a three-dimensional, visual image of the functional processes of the brain. A PET scan can make it possible to see what is happening in the brain and show the areas that are in use at a particular time and with a specific context. The PET scan was used on people who had been diagnosed with Asperger syndrome[1] and people who were not affected by Asperger syndrome. What they discovered was particularly enlightening, giving an insight into the differences in thought processing between the NT partner and the partner with Asperger syndrome. All participants in both groups were asked two questions regarding the story they had been told. One question only required logical, general knowledge abilities. The other question required that participants have insight into another's mind. For the group who were not affected by Asperger syndrome, two very separate regions of the brain were shown to activate on the PET scan in response to the two questions asked.

In order to answer the question that required theory of mind, an area in the centre of the prefrontal cortex was activated. The prefrontal cortex is one of the most advanced areas of the brain and along with other areas of the brain plays a major part in the development of theory of mind. Theory of mind is an ability to separate the thoughts, beliefs and opinions of another from our own and is generated by the part of the brain that governs empathy, mindreading and insight into another's mind.

---

1   At the time of this study, Asperger syndrome was the recognized term used by the *Diagnostic and Statistical Manual of Mental Disorders, Fourth Edition* to describe individuals on the milder end of the spectrum. This term has now been replaced with autistic spectrum condition level one by the *DSM-5*. The *DSM* is a manual published by the American Psychiatric Association. It lists all the relevant symptoms for a diagnosis of each disorder.

This area of the brain did not activate on the PET scan, when the group affected by AS were asked the question that required having insight into another's mind. Instead, the logical, general cognitive part of the brain became active – the same part of the brain that had been used to work out the general knowledge question.

This suggests that the AS participants were attempting to understand another person's mind state using logic. The problem is that people are not necessarily logical when it comes to thoughts, beliefs or behaviour. Although the AS group managed to answer the question, it took a lot longer than the non-AS group, as it was approached like working out a crossword puzzle. It is therefore likely that if the AS participants had been under pressure to answer quickly they could have given an incorrect answer (unless they had experienced a similar situation and were able to recall an appropriate answer). It takes much longer for AS individuals to find an answer for a question that requires insight and mindreading, when applying logic rather than theory of mind.

This does not suggest that the AS participants had no theory of mind, but it may suggest that theory of mind had not fully developed. A typical developing four-year-old child would be able to pass tests on the ability to apply theory of mind, whereas with children affected by autism, theory of mind does not begin to develop until the child is between 9 and 14 years old (Happé and Frith 1995). This implies that in children affected by autism, awareness that other people have different mind states, separate from their own, may never develop beyond the very basic level. It is unlikely that development will ever fully progress to the second stage of understanding – that of appreciating that other people actually have their own separate thoughts and feelings (Happé and Frith 1995).

An underdeveloped theory of mind has been proposed as the core deficit in autism, and its impact has been found at all developmental levels throughout the life span (Ozonoff, Roger and Pennington 1991). The development of theory of mind is essential in order to empathize spontaneously with another; to see and understand the perspective of another; to relate to another's state of mind; and to understand that another's mind state is separate from one's own. This does not mean the AS partner cannot care or show sympathy (sympathy and empathy are two quite different things), as the majority of the AS partners I encounter can be very sympathetic, especially if the situation demands practical help and support. However, they will not be able automatically to understand and experience another person's feelings while separating them from their own unless time is taken to explain to them in a clear and logical way how their partner feels. It is this difference in empathetic abilities that will have the greatest impact on a couple's relationship as it will be responsible for most of the misunderstandings, consequently leading to both struggling to understand what it is that keeps breaking down between them.

Another important aspect of these differences will be the impact on the partners individually, particularly on the AS partner, as they will be trying to work out everything by applying logic. For example, when the AS partner enters a room full of people or joins a group situation, they will not only be trying to work out the environment applying logic, but they will also be trying to use logic to work out the people they encounter. The AS partner's brain will have to work very hard to keep up with the speed of conversation in a group situation. In a more intimate or emotional situation, the AS partner will struggle with many of the nuances of communication, as will often occur when the AS partner is with the NT partner. The AS partner's brain will be trying to apply logic to the facial expressions, body language and intonation of language, often falling behind as trying to think of suitable responses will cause delay. Distractions such as peripheral movement or background noises will also impinge on the AS partner. The list goes on and on.

It is no wonder that the AS partner can find themselves quickly overloaded or in meltdown. There is basically too much emotional information for the logical brain to process and adequately respond to. If the AS partner or others involved in the situation do not recognize this potential meltdown in time and make an effort to call a halt to what is happening, then the AS partner's brain will reach a point of total overload. The brain will then assume it is under threat and in defence will send the AS partner into one of three possible responses: fight, flight or freeze. A fight response will be highly defensive and can be quite antagonistic; it may include verbal abuse, shouting, banging or breaking objects, and slamming doors. A flight response can involve walking out, abandoning a partner at a social event and turning off all forms of contact such as phones and computers. The third response is the freeze response. Freeze is being totally immobilized, in complete shutdown, like a rabbit caught in the headlights, unable to move or function, scared to speak, react or escape for fear of confrontation. I have found this fear of confrontation to affect the majority of the AS clients I have worked with. All responses are survival strategies and would be very useful in a life-threatening situation, but none is very useful in a relationship situation and probably results in doing more harm than good. I will discuss meltdowns in more detail in Chapter 5.

It is very likely that after a meltdown the AS partner's recollection of what happened may be different from what actually happened, potentially sparking off another heated discussion between the AS partner and the NT partner. The NT partner may believe the AS partner is not being honest or is trying to change the truth. This is not necessarily the case as, due to stress and the overload in the AS partner's brain, information will have been lost. This will not be because of the AS partner's failure to remember, but because the data never reached the AS partner's long-term memory. Both the AS partner and the NT partner may have a very different perspective of what happened. This can be confusing and frustrating for both of them. It can have a detrimental effect on the trust between them, especially if either believes the other is being dishonest or manipulating the truth.

Autism or personality

When a couple are aware that their relationship is affected by autism it can be quite difficult to decipher what traits are caused by personality and what are due to being on the autistic spectrum. Not all differences are due to the partner being on the autistic spectrum, and not all personality traits can be attributed to, or in some cases blamed on, autism.

During my time working with couples I frequently find myself saying one of two things to the NT partner. This is either 'No, your partner is not able to do that, because if they could, they would not be on the spectrum!' or 'No, you cannot blame autism for that, it has nothing to do with being on the spectrum. It is because of who they are.'

For example, if the NT partner states that she shouldn't have to explain how she feels because her partner should 'just know' automatically, then I will explain that this expectation is unfair to their partner and would be the same as saying to someone affected by dyslexia that they should automatically know how to always spell correctly! In the same way, if the NT partner stated the reason her partner was violent towards her was because he had autism, then I would explain that that is not the case and behaving violently towards someone is not an autistic trait.

Knowing whether a trait is caused by having autism or personality is confusing for both in a couple relationship, especially the NT partner. One of the reasons it is so confusing is because everyone on the spectrum is so different, all will have their own unique personality, their own childhood history, which will in many ways have moulded who they are now and will have encouraged certain beliefs, behaviours and opinions. Attachment style will also play a part in how a child develops, and this will be reflected in the relationships they form in adulthood.

On the following pages, I have put together a questionnaire for each partner to answer separately. The aim of the questionnaire is to allow the couple to explore what is and what is not a trait due to having autism. The questions are closed and require a Yes or No answer. So, for example, if you think having autism will make a person more likely to be flirtatious, then tick Yes; if not, then tick No. There is not a maybe answer here, so if you really don't know, choose the answer you think is most likely and put a question mark rather than a tick. The answers are supplied after the questionnaire.

▬ Instructions for the AS and NT partner

Look through the list below.

1. Tick Yes if you believe a trait is caused by having autism.

2. Tick No if you believe a trait is NOT caused by having autism.

3. If you are not sure, then put a question mark in the column you feel is most likely.

4. When you have both completed a questionnaire, check with the answers on the following page; share your answers together.

5. Explore topics such as:
   - Did you answer the same?
   - Did any of the answers surprise you?
   - Are there any answers that will change how you feel?

WORKSHEET
What trait is caused by being on the spectrum?

		YES	NO			YES	NO
1	Flirtatious			21	Clumsy		
2	Unfaithful			22	Intuitive		
3	Inhibited			23	Passionate		
4	Frigid			24	Logical		
5	Promiscuous			25	Irrational		
6	Violent			26	Rigid/inflexible		
7	Verbally abusive			27	Impulsive		
8	Boring			28	Reactive to noise/smell/touch/taste/light		
9	A trainspotter						
10	Reliable			29	Defensive		
11	Emotionally withdrawn			30	Critical		
12	Withholding			31	Pedantic		
13	Highly focused			32	Opinionated		
14	Single minded			33	Religious		
15	Self-centred			34	Political		
16	Unsympathetic			35	An unloving parent		
17	Stingy			36	Forgetful		
18	Obsessive			37	A loner		
19	Unhygienic			38	Generous		
20	Unkempt			39	Extravagant		

Answers: Traits due to being on the spectrum: 13, 14, 18, 21, 24, 26, 28, 31.

Discuss together when you have some private quiet time to spare. As can be seen, very few of the traits can be attributed to being affected by autism. If a trait is discovered to be due to personality, then it is more likely that it can be changed, and this can offer hope for a couple. It is also worth remembering that autism is a spectrum, so the severity of the traits that affect an individual can vary greatly. For instance, in the case of sensory sensitivity, I have worked with clients who find this aspect almost debilitating, while others are only affected mildly when their stress levels are running high.

Equally, there are some traits, such as a strong defensive reaction to any perceived criticism, that will appear to affect the majority of individuals on the spectrum. However, a defensive reaction is not directly due to autism, as this, with awareness and the desire to improve the relationship, can be changed.

If a trait is due to being on the spectrum, then it may be more difficult to change, and any change will not be maintainable as it will never be natural. For example, an AS person can learn that if their partner cries, they need a hug, but they will not be able to automatically know when this rule has changed and a hug is the last thing their partner needs. They will only know this if they are given advance warning and clear instructions. This is not always easy for the NT partner to do, especially when feeling upset or angry. For many, to objectively clarify their needs when in a state of heightened emotions is out of their reach, especially as their AS partner, who is probably becoming quite anxious trying to get it right, might become defensive and argue back from a very different perspective.

A different perspective

There have been times in my work as a counsellor when I have been told differing accounts of the same situation by a couple, both together in the room, that were so opposing it was difficult to believe that they shared the same context. This can make my work quite confusing at times because I cannot deny either of their experiences and have to accept both accounts as true. This truth, however, is based on each individual client's perspective of how they heard, saw and interpreted the situation when it happened. The brain can be very selective in what it chooses to process and store in its long-term memory banks, and memory is often focused on what is most relevant to each partner in the relationship, especially if either is feeling insecure, threatened or defensive.

To understand how a couple can be in the same place at the same time and yet have such different perspectives, imagine two people standing back to back on the top of a mountain. One is the NT partner and the other the AS partner. Each will focus on what is most relevant and of interest to them. The AS partner's attention is caught by the view of a city and consists of buildings, trains, cars and factories. The NT partner's view is captivated by the colour of the countryside, a running river, wildlife and a beautiful meadow. Both are stood in the same place at the same time and yet both are seeing very different views, so their respective perceptions of the same place are radically different. Later when they discuss it, both are surprised and taken aback by the different memory they both have of the experience and will struggle to figure out why their respective perspectives are so different. If at this point in the communication either partner challenges the other on their differing perspective, it could cause a very defensive reaction, as it will feel as though they are being belittled, not believed and ultimately being called a liar.

This is how different perspectives can cause major misunderstandings if the couple are not aware that neither is lying or being manipulative but simply seeing things from a different point of view. However, just because they are aware that they see things differently or accept that they process information differently, this does not mean it will be any easier for the couple to deal with the misunderstandings. It is useful to understand why the difference exists – understanding can make such a difference to the relationship and the self-esteem of both. In therapy, I find the first and most relevant area that needs to be addressed is a couple's different communication methods and how each needs to learn a way of understanding the other's language.

Chapter 2

COMMUNICATION

COMMUNICATION is the area often highlighted as the root cause of most of the problems in the relationship. A couple may report a history of misunderstandings, feeling unheard, feeling criticized and not getting the point. Over a period of time this may have resulted in the AS partner refusing to communicate at all, especially if they feel the subject matter is going to lead to a confrontation. For the AS partner, there is likely to be a history of unintentionally getting it wrong and they may have learned that it is far better not to say anything at all. For the NT partner, this reluctance to communicate or express feelings could be read as rejection and a lack of caring, increasing the NT partner's frustration. The AS partner may pick up on this frustration and interpret it as anger, without knowing why their partner is angry, thus leading to the AS partner withdrawing further, and so the cycle goes on. Here is a case study that illustrates this well.

● CASE STUDY: DAVID AND AMY

David (aged 42) and Amy (aged 39) had been married for nine years and they had a son who was four years old and a daughter who was two years old. Before the birth of her son, Amy worked full time as a couple counsellor. She had always prided herself on her excellent communication abilities; however, her abilities appeared to be completely useless when she tried to communicate her feelings with David who worked long hours as an accountant. Sometimes David would not arrive home until 8pm or later, long after Amy had put the children to bed. Any intimacy or affection between them was almost non-existent, and every time they tried to discuss the issues that bothered them an argument ensued. Both had been feeling very neglected, unappreciated and miserable for a long time.

The day in question had been particularly bad for Amy – everything that could go wrong had. Their son had had a tantrum in the supermarket because he wanted his favourite chicken burgers and there weren't any. Their daughter had been sick in the supermarket cafeteria and her new dress was covered in regurgitated chocolate yogurt. The restaurant staff were anything but helpful or sympathetic and, as if this wasn't enough, on returning home Amy found the washing machine had broken down in the middle of a cycle and refused to return any of its half-washed garments as the door would not unlock. By the time David arrived home after 8pm, Amy felt totally exhausted.

David had not had a great day either and had spent the majority of it dealing with a very difficult and argumentative client who seemed to expect David to break all the rules and work miracles with his company's business accounts!

David came home still playing over the conversations with his awkward client in his head; he was not feeling great, and without announcing himself or seeking Amy out, he went straight into the kitchen and made himself a strong cup of coffee. He sat at the kitchen table needing time to adjust and collect his thoughts together.

Amy, who had been upstairs trying to settle the children down for the third time, entered the kitchen, feeling exhausted, tired and totally spent. She didn't notice David at first, but when she did, she jumped, as she did not know he was there.

Below is how the communication passed between them.

'Oh, good grief, I didn't know you were home! How long have you been sat there?' This question was meant by Amy as a genuine enquiry, but her surprised voice and startled body language did not support this.

David immediately felt under attack, not dissimilar to how he had been feeling all day with his client, but was unable to react due to his high professional standards. David reacted aggressively and defensively: 'Oh for goodness sake Amy, give me a break, don't start on me as soon as I come home. I've had the day from hell!'

Amy reacted just as aggressively back: 'Day from hell! *You've* had a day from hell! What about *my* day! You don't have a clue what goes on for me! You never ask what sort of day I have had...' Amy continued to express her pent-up feelings for quite a long time, releasing all the frustration, discontentment and sheer aloneness she had been storing for months.

'This is so unfair...' David tried to say but didn't get far before Amy interjected again. 'My marriage to you is unfair, you never show me any appreciation or care. In fact, I don't think you do care about me anymore, I don't know why we stay together!'

Rather than realizing this was a cry for help from Amy, who was feeling very neglected and unappreciated, this exclamation interpreted itself to David as Amy saying 'I want a divorce'. David, now feeling very insecure and criticized, shouted back at Amy, 'So this is all about you wanting a divorce. So you think I am useless, a failure as a husband. I might as well leave now!', at which David banged his drink down on the table and walked out of the front door, slamming it so hard behind him that it woke the children up from their slumber.

The evening was finished for David and Amy – both felt devastated and wrecked. David did not come back until after work the following day. He had turned off his phone and Amy was desperately worried about him. Both felt mortally wounded and as if there was no way back as too much had been said. Neither could even remember what initially caused it, but both felt convinced it was the other who was to blame. This case study shows how David misread Amy's original intent in her opening statement and heard it as direct criticism rather than an enquiry. All this could have been avoided if some rules and strategies had been put in place beforehand, or if the issues that had been building up for both had been communicated before they reached boiling point.

David and Amy did manage to sort out their issues with the help of a couple therapist. It took much time, patience and commitment from both to change their communication methods. They put in new rules and learned to be totally congruent with each other and communicate if they felt unappreciated or unloved. It was initially hard work to change the destructive pattern that had developed between them and replace it with a new healthy pattern of communication and mutual support.

Just as learning to communicate openly and honestly with each other is essential in maintaining a healthy relationship, sometimes knowing when not to communicate can be equally beneficial.

When not to communicate

There is a time and a place for everything, and if you are in an AS/NT relationship that rule applies very strongly to communication. Just as time and thought have to be given to when to communicate issues of importance or feelings and emotions, there will equally be a very definite time when not to communicate, and it is worth taking time to put this rule into place together and agree how it will be applied. Dealing with silence can feel very uncomfortable for many people. One of the reasons for this is that silence may have been used as a punishment for them in the past. Another reason is that the AS partner, who may struggle with reading body language, will have little to monitor their partner by if they do not speak. Silence, or stonewalling as it is commonly referred to when used to purposely punish or confuse another, is a very powerful and cruel way to exercise control over another. If this is happening in your relationship, then you might both wish to seek the help of a therapist to help resolve the underlying issues that are causal to this negative pattern of behaviour.

Silence, if used sensitively and correctly, however, can be very beneficial and at times a relationship saver if used for the right reasons. For example, thinking back to the case study of David and Amy, far less damage would have been inflicted on their relationship if it had been recognized that silence would have been the better alternative for both until time had been taken to process their thoughts and destress from their busy day. However, this would only work if it had been prearranged and mutually agreed between both.

Various ways can be employed to convey to the other partner that a time of silence is required. Here are a few suggestions, but bear in mind that it is important to find what works for both partners.

Do something that helps to feel calm and destress

A partner states they have something they need to do, such as:

- Walk the dog

- Sit in the garden

- Do some gardening

- Catch up on the news

- Fix something

- Clean the car

- Prepare/cook/wash/iron something

- Have a shower/shave/bath

- Go to the toilet.

These are all statements that can be prearranged beforehand with the other partner which indicate the need for some time alone (up to 30 minutes) to not communicate, collect their thoughts and find a sense of calm. The other partner will then need to occupy themselves for the duration of this time and try not to disturb their partner's time-out.

Have a sign or a signal

This can be anything that works. A lady with AS once described to me how she used the characters from *Winnie the Pooh*. If she needed silent time out, she would put a toy/model of Eeyore on the shelf in clear view of her partner so he would know she needed a small period of silent time. When she felt okay and ready to communicate, Eeyore would be replaced with Tigger. This worked really well for them, and the characters can be substituted by whatever you prefer or can relate to.

Send a text or a WhatsApp message

Oh, the joy of the emoji! I am convinced they were created by people on the spectrum, for people on the spectrum. One little picture can replace so many words needed to explain feelings verbally and thus minimize feelings of anxiety in the talker and avoiding a defensive reaction in the receiver. Examples of emojis are plentiful to represent 'needing some silent time', such as the silent or shush emoji. There are so many to choose from – pick one together which works for both of you.

You might prefer just to text the word 'space'. Whatever you use, it would be beneficial to put a 'kiss' x in the text to add reassurance and soften the message. Using this or other strategies to communicate the need for silent time can make life easier and less complicated, as long as three important rules are followed:

1. The strategy is arranged beforehand.

2. Whatever strategy you employ, it must work for both of you.

3. Silent time-out is no longer than 30 minutes.

Planning ahead

Autism and spontaneity do not mix well, and sudden change can cause anxiety and stress for the AS partner. Coping skills and relationship strategies need to be planned beforehand, and although this might sound like hard work, it will in the long run prevent misunderstandings, confusion and meltdowns. Equally, strategies and relationship rules must be negotiated and mutually agreed by both partners together.

Unless more or less time has been agreed, 30 minutes should be ample time to spend in silence. Silence continued for too long can become destructive and feel rejecting, rather than beneficial to the couple. Just to clarify that silence refers to a couple not verbally communicating – it does not mean that you are not allowed to make any noise. For example, one of my AS clients would find a place to quietly play his guitar, as he found this relaxing. Equally, an NT client might choose to listen to an audio book or the radio. As long as the sound does not disturb or aggravate the other partner then it can be a good way for both to relax. Using strategies and putting them into place will take time and patience. At times, it can feel like learning a new language, just as a couple would do if they came from different cultures. Understanding and accepting the differences is essential if a couple are going to improve their understanding of each other's different communication style.

It will take time, patience and commitment by the couple to change their communication methods. It will be hard work as a pattern will have evolved between the couple that will make it quite difficult for them to spot the triggers which cause the communication failures. Finding an appropriate therapist to work on communication with them can feel less critical for the couple, as the therapist can act as an unbiased third party, observe the interactions between the couple and reflect back to them where improvements could be made. It is often easier to hear this from someone impartial whom the couple are comfortable with and whose observations won't be taken personally.

However, if it has not been possible to find a therapist to work with, a couple can use the worksheets in this book and experiment together until a way can be found that works for both of them.

Communicating on different wavelengths

The first step in improving communication is to understand why it breaks down in the first place. I use the analogy of wavelengths to describe this. Imagine two transceivers, both able to receive and transmit information, where, unbeknown to either, their wavelengths are different. One is tuned for logical FM while the other is tuned for emotional FM. Logical FM suits the AS partner as it works in a linear way, transmitting one message at a time and receiving from one transmitter at a time. Emotional FM suits the NT partner as it works in an unpredictable way, transmitting multiple messages and receiving from multiple transmitters. Both are using the same waveband (FM), but neither is capable of the tuning required to interpret messages from the other transmitter.

Logical transmission versus emotional transmission

Imagine two transceivers – the first one can only transmit and receive on a logical wavelength; the transmissions will be linear, one subject at a time and have a beginning and an end.

The second transceiver transmits in a very different way – it uses an emotional wavelength. This is quite different to the former and consists of ups and downs, zigzags and loops. It can transmit many messages at the same time and does not have a precise beginning or end.

When these two transmitters try to communicate, the result is going to be a complete breakdown in communication, leaving both feeling unheard and misunderstood.

One thing at a time

The example of the two transceivers illustrates well an important aspect in the difference between the AS partner and the NT partner's communication style. Besides communicating on a different wavelength, there is a further difference in how the two transmitters receive their messages. The logical transmitter will only be able to send and receive one message at a time; if multiple messages are being transmitted, then it is highly likely that either the point of the message will be totally missed and/or important elements of the message will not be remembered. This is quite different from the emotional transmitter of the NT partner who will be able to deal with multiple messages and easily manage them all. Sometimes it is hard for the NT partner to understand why this ability is not shared between them, and their expectations may exceed their partner's abilities. If this is voiced in an undermining, insensitive way, it can cause much damage to their partner's self-esteem and cause them to communicate even less.

As well as avoiding multiple messages, the AS partner may also struggle with the problem of distraction. If we stay with the example of the logical linear wavelength which represents the AS transmitter, distraction could be likened to tuning that wavelength out and away from its original station. Hence the messages being received would be illegible and incomprehensible as the AS transmitter had tuned into another station. The majority of NT clients I see are often already aware that their AS partner struggles with multitasking, but not always aware of how easily they can be distracted or tuned out by noises or movements that are happening around them. I have a clock in my therapy room that often finds itself outside in reception as a client will have found it difficult to concentrate on what was being said as they were constantly tuning in to the ticking of the clock. Sometimes this tuning out of the conversation is not always caused by an external nuance – it might be an internal thought. For example, if the AS partner is in the middle of doing something or about to say something, I recommend that they are given the time to complete the task before any important information is communicated. If not, even though it might appear that their attention is being offered, they will be rehearsing what it is they need to do, say or complete in their internal thought processor.

The NT partner should be aware of any distractions when communicating with their AS partner as they can disrupt communication and make misunderstandings more likely. The AS partner may have tuned in to a distraction and not be receiving the message which the NT partner is sending. Messages given in this state are in danger of being lost or misunderstood by the AS partner. When the purpose of the message is raised later, the AS partner may appear to have completely forgotten what was said, and this can lead to disagreements. The NT partner could, first, believe that the AS partner was not bothered about what was said and had dismissed it as irrelevant because it was said by the NT partner or, second, that the AS partner made a conscious decision to annoy the NT partner and ignore their message. Neither of these assumptions would be correct and both partners will be left feeling hurt and confused. Situations like these can be avoided if thought and effort are given to the context in which a message is being given.

Applying and following some simple rules that both partners agree to can help to improve the situation. Add your own to the end of the list.

■ Rules for giving important messages

Important messages should not be given when:

- the radio or television is on
- the AS partner is working on the computer, reading or concentrating on something else
- either partner is in a hurry to go somewhere
- the children or other family members are making demands on either partner
- either partner is feeling stressed
- the AS partner has just arrived home from work
- the family or partners are eating
- either partner is driving the car
- in a group situation such as a dinner party or while out with friends
- in any noisy or chaotic environment.

Getting the AS partner's attention

If the NT partner wants to be certain their message is being received, then they will need to be sure they have their partner's attention before they deliver their message to them, otherwise there is a grave risk it will not be heard or heard accurately. One way of doing this is to always use the AS partner's name at the beginning of the message. This really useful strategy was offered by Wenn Lawson at a conference I attended. Wenn, who has autism and wrote the informative book *Sex, Sexuality and the Autistic Spectrum* (2005), recommended that having used the person's name to open the message, they should count to ten and then repeat the person's name followed by the message. Lawson explained that this time was needed for the person with autism to make the transition in their brain from what they were doing to receiving the message. Lawson did suggest that counting to ten was dependent on the person receiving the message and could be adapted if a longer or shorter count was needed.

Memory aids

Another successful strategy that can be applied to ensure messages are received and remembered is the use of physical reminders which the AS partner either can refer to or is automatically prompted to. This not only makes important messages more concrete but also gives the AS partner a tool to aid memory. Reminders that can be used are:

- mobile calendar apps and reminders
- mobile phone alerts
- post-it notes
- written lists
- emails
- whiteboards
- noticeboards.

As I said earlier, there is no guarantee that a given method will work for a given couple, so I always advise a couple to experiment and find out what works best for them. I have found that as well as using memory aids, it is equally important where they are placed. Calendars are good for putting down appointments and birthdays, but often that calendar is tucked away in a corner or up high on the wall. Equally, whiteboards cannot be taken to work with you, and emails are only useful if the person is going to look on their computer or phone, and some jobs prohibit the use of either. If the AS partner uses the car to drive to and from work, then sticking a post-it note to the dashboard (take it down while driving) is useful because it will be seen. One lady attached a post-it note to her purse as it was something she was guaranteed to look at. Mobile phone calendars and organizers are excellent as a memory aid and can be set to alert the owner anything from ten minutes to a week before the important upcoming event. It will be by trial and error that a couple will work out what works best for them.

As well as considering how to get a partner's attention and how to ensure that the message has been heard, understood and will be retained, there is also the consideration of how the message is delivered. All too often important messages are overloaded and given as statements with no indication as to what is expected in response. This can leave the partner on the spectrum feeling quite bewildered as to what is expected of them next, what they are supposed to do and whether they are expected to reply. Using the whole sentence strategy (Aston 2001) can eliminate the confusion and ambiguity which overflows in our frequently hasty exchanges.

Whole-sentence strategy

Using whole sentences slows down the sometimes erratic pace in conversations as they require a little thought to piece together; this is especially true if there has been a misunderstanding or an overreaction. For example, having had an unexpected overreaction from their partner, either partner should try and apply whole, single sentences to the situation; for example, 'I can see what I have just said has upset you. That was not my intention. Can you explain to me what it is that upset you?' Further application of this whole-sentence strategy can be seen in the following examples.

Example 1: Avoiding the 'you' word

On the way home after an evening out at a very expensive restaurant, where the NT partner became unhappy with their AS partner's attitude to others, he says, 'Did you have to be so rude to everyone? I cannot believe how you spoke to that waitress. You ruined the whole evening by your stupid childish tantrum!'

The use of 'you' in an argumentative tone is often heard as direct criticism and can be antagonistic. Applying whole sentences without the use of the word 'you' can help keep the situation calmer. Our NT partner could have said, 'I realize how annoying the waitress was after we had waited so long for our meal. However, I felt very embarrassed by some of the things that were said. Can we discuss how we might find a better way of dealing with this in the future?'

Example 2: Picking an appropriate moment

The AS partner has just walked in from work. The television is on, the children are playing up and the dog wants to go out. The NT partner is annoyed and says, 'How could you forget you were meeting me at the school? You do not give a damn about getting this statement for Thomas. All you care about is your work. I may as well be a single parent. At least I would get the extra support.'

It is likely that the AS partner had completely forgotten the appointment and is totally bemused by the situation; they have only just arrived home and there's a good chance they will withdraw back out again, escaping with the dog. A more appropriate time to discuss this may have been later in the evening, after the children have gone to bed. The NT partner could say, 'I was expecting us to meet at the school today to discuss Thomas's statement. I felt very alone without you. I wonder if it's worth starting to use a diary/computer/phone alert?'

Example 3: Being sensitive to the situation

The AS partner has just come home from work. The NT partner is busy cooking dinner in the kitchen. Having noticed the hall is a bit messy, the AS partner says, 'I see the hall floor needs vacuuming.' Not a very flattering hello, and from it the NT partner will have probably heard, 'What have you been doing all day?'

Arriving home is an important time of coming back together as a couple/family. Neither partner knows what sort of day the other has had. Therefore, an initial friendly or loving greeting does help. It would be better if the AS partner did not mention the hall floor at all. However, once something has been noticed, the AS partner will find it very hard not to mention it. So, a kinder, more considerate way might have been: 'Hello dear/sweetheart (kiss). You have been busy. Shall I give the hall floor a quick vac round while you finish dinner?'

Example 4: Saying what you mean

A couple is going out for the evening. The NT partner has just finished getting ready when the AS partner enters the bedroom and says, 'Are you going to get ready then? We're due there at 7.30.'

This is not a good start to the evening. It is likely that the AS partner either had something else in mind for the NT partner to wear or simply hadn't noticed they had changed. If the AS partner does have something in mind, then perhaps they could say, 'You're looking lovely. I was hoping you would wear (particular item) tonight. I really like you in that.'

These four examples, two for each partner to consider, highlight how the NT partner, being more emotionally adept, is prone to over-elaborate but is able to pause and reword what they want to say, while the AS partner, being more logically adept, does not say enough but can learn that certain situations, like arriving home, need certain responses.

Another major factor that can cause memory lapses is stress. The more stressed the AS partner becomes, the more they will struggle with memory and communication. This can make the AS partner appear more affected by autism. Keeping stress to a minimum is beneficial to all concerned. One cause of stress for the AS partner can be when they are expected or are being pressured to express their feelings or to work out someone else's feelings.

The card communication system

Making the relationship between an AS partner and an NT partner work will mean the couple experimenting until they find ways to communicate – in a way that they can both understand and translate correctly – otherwise communication will continue to fail. This means that both have to become more aware of each other's differences and try to accept and work with them rather than trying to change them.

The AS partner can be very sensitive to perceived criticism and has probably had a lifetime's experience of having 'got it wrong' going right back to their childhood. The AS partner will be inclined to hear criticism where none is intended. The AS partner needs to be aware of their sensitivity and make a real effort to check with their NT partner when they perceive they are being criticized. The AS partner needs to be able to ask the NT partner to be more specific about what they are saying. The AS partner needs to try and resist the instinct to shut down or become defensive before the NT partner has had the chance to explain what they are really trying to say.

The NT partner will be trying to learn a new way of communicating, learning to use logic rather than emotion with their partner. There is no easy solution, but one way of doing this is to change the medium by which the message is conveyed, using visual forms of communication rather than words.

Let me explain. A difficult and sensitive issue has been raised which, due to poor reception and translation, has been lost. Both partners are feeling frustrated at not being understood, and if it continues someone may lose their temper or say something they will regret. The NT partner, in their frustration, may turn and say, 'I've had enough of this! I am tired of trying to explain. Why does something so simple become such hard work for me? I can only think it is because you do not care enough to try and understand!'

The NT partner would like the AS partner to respond, 'Of course I care, I am trying to understand. Let's just have a hug for now and come back to this later.' Unfortunately, it is more likely that the AS partner will have heard this as direct criticism, interpreting it as 'My partner thinks I am stupid and a failure as a partner.' This is all part of the transmitter not being able to receive and translate the message correctly, especially since by now the AS partner is teetering on the edge of a meltdown.

The AS partner is likely to walk away with a brain that feels as if it is going to explode from emotional overload, having reached a point of either being unable to find the words or fearing that whatever they say at this point will be the wrong thing. This will reinforce the NT partner's view that the AS partner does not care enough to resolve the issue and does not even want to try. The NT partner may shout after the AS partner that if the AS partner walks away one more time the relationship is over, thus reinforcing the AS partner's perception that the NT partner cannot stand them and wants out of the relationship.

The relationship may become insecure and distrustful and the self-esteem of both partners may be plummeting. The original issue will not be raised or resolved, as both will feel too fragile to return to it for fear of repeating the same communication breakdown. This is an example of an absolute breakdown between the couple. This could have been avoided by using what I call a carding system. If we take the scenario at the point where the AS partner was becoming confused or unsure of what the NT partner was saying, they could have said, 'This is a yellow card situation.' This would signal to the NT partner to pause and track back to a point where the AS partner is able to say, 'This is a green card situation', green card meaning they understand what the discussion is about, allowing them to then continue the discussion. This use of yellow and green cards will, it is hoped, help the couple to avoid that absolute breakdown.

However, if the situation does reach the point where frustrations are expressed negatively, then that partner should be able to say, 'This is a red card situation', rather than the potentially hurtful or destructive words they might use. The discussion then ends but the door is left open for it to resume at a later time or date without recriminations on either side.

Words are easy to misinterpret, especially in the heat of an argument. This system uses cards instead of words, and these cards can be shown or spoken. The use of the green card can be helpful as it tells the other partner, 'I'm okay, I understand', while the yellow card says, 'I'm not sure. Can you try and explain differently?' If the situation manages to go beyond these, then the red card allows for that pause without the situation degenerating further.

Example of the card communication system

Red card stands for Danger.

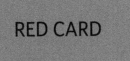

We need to stop this debate right now. We cannot sort this out at the moment.

I am frightened this will get out of control. I am too upset to continue.

I do not want to say anything that will hurt you.

Yellow card stands for Uncertainty.

YELLOW CARD

I do not fully understand what you mean.

Please tell me in a way that I can understand. Can you go back and explain again, please?

I am unsure as to what you want me to do.

Green card means I am okay.

GREEN CARD

I understand what you are saying.

I feel okay with what you have told me.

▪ Instructions for using the card system

1. Decide exactly what you both want each card to mean.

2. Agree together situations that you might use the card system for.

3. Decide whether you would rather use an actual card or just say, 'This is a ... card situation!'

4. If the red card is called, then both must respect this and allow the other time-out.

5. An arrangement to re-address the situation will need to be made so it is not just ignored, as unresolved issues do not go away.

WORKSHEET
Card communication system

Red card stands for Danger.

RED CARD

Put your own card meanings:

Yellow card stands for Uncertainty.

YELLOW CARD

Put your own card meanings:

Green card means I am okay.

GREEN CARD

Put your own card meanings:

It is important the card system is not used as a way of totally avoiding particular topics or issues. The red card does not mean the subject is closed. It needs to be understood by both that they will return to the subject at a later date which suits both. Ignored issues are unresolved issues, and unresolved issues come back to haunt, so they will need to be addressed at some point. If the couple are in therapy, then they can take the unresolved issue to the therapy session where, in an environment safe for both, the therapist may be able to offer different perspectives or strategies for them.

The card communication system can be used at different times for different reasons. It is a way of letting the other person know clearly how each feels without the use of words, which may be interpreted as hurtful or rejecting. The system can be used to let the other partner know or reassure them that sense is being made of what's being said and that things are okay. When something feels ambiguous or one partner feels they are missing the point, then the system can also help. With practice, the card communication system will soon become a habit and leave less room for ambiguity and misunderstanding.

The topic of communication can also make a major difference as to how well the AS partner will respond to and recall what is said. If the communication is logical and not overloaded with ambiguities, there will rarely be a problem, especially if it is about or linked to their special interest. However, in relationship communication, the topic will vary greatly and often will not be a logical interest-focused one – it will be about feelings and emotions that need to be aired and discussed. It is these intimate conversations that will frequently break down and can either end quite abruptly, or escalate into an argument, if not handled sensitively and at a sensitive pace. The AS partner will need time to process and respond to questions without being put under pressure. It is often these emotionally loaded conversations that are responsible for one of the partners having a meltdown. Overloaded, intimate and emotional conversations can quickly fall apart, leaving the AS partner feeling under pressure and the NT partner frustrated that their point is not understood and their partner just doesn't 'get it'. There are ways and strategies to help avoid this and make life easier for both partners and other family members. One way can be to fully understand why discussing emotions can be so profoundly difficult for some individuals on the spectrum.

Chapter 3

EXPRESSING FEELINGS AND ALEXITHYMIA

What is alexithymia?

Awareness by clinicians of the existence of alexithymia first came about in the 1970s. It was not until the 1990s that links were contemplated between alexithymia and an autistic spectrum condition. Alexithymia is a Greek term meaning (literally) 'without words for feelings'. It is the inability to express or interpret emotions and moods in the self as indicated by bodily sensations or to understand and value another's emotions and moods.

Who does alexithymia affect?

Alexithymia can affect children and adults alike. As well as being found in individuals with autism, alexithymia also affects individuals suffering from:

- post-traumatic stress disorder
- depression
- Parkinson's disease
- multiple sclerosis
- schizophrenia
- eating disorders
- substance abuse.

What percentage of AS individuals are affected by alexithymia?

A study in Finland showed that alexithymia affected 13 per cent of the general population and that men were almost twice as likely to be affected by it compared with women (Salminen *et al.* 1999). In individuals with an ASC, the percentage with alexithymia was found to be considerably higher, at over 50 per cent (Hill, Berthoz and Frith 2004).

What are the symptoms of alexithymia?

Symptoms and their severity can fluctuate among individuals as alexithymia, like autism, is a spectrum condition.

Symptoms include:

- in children, a lack of imagination in play and fantasy

- a lack of ability to translate emotions and moods experienced by self into words

- difficulty understanding and responding appropriately to another's emotions

- difficulty in applying empathy.

How is alexithymia assessed?

As alexithymia is not regarded as a mental health disorder it does not appear in the latest version of the *Diagnostic and Statistical Manual of Mental Disorders, Fifth Edition* (*DSM-5*) (American Psychiatric Association 2013). However, there are tests for an individual to complete online if they suspect they may be affected by alexithymia. Assessment is largely by self-report and is often determined by the assessor listening to the language and words used by the individual being assessed when describing feelings. It may become very apparent to the assessor that describing or discussing feelings is totally avoided or extremely limited. It can also be observed that the individual being assessed shows a lack of understanding of and insight into the emotions and moods of others.

Alexithymia and empathy

Over the many years of working with clients on the spectrum I have become more aware of the diversity in their capacity not just to describe their feelings but also to give empathetic responses towards their partners' pain or distress.

I have listened to NT partners describe being left alone at home or not provided with adequate food, let alone any tender loving care when they have been sick or injured. While alternatively, I have heard glowing reports from NT partners in the same situation being cared for, nurtured and provided with an abundance of sympathy from their partners. The difference was quite astounding, and although in some cases it could be observed as a direct consequence of personality differences, I was often of the opinion that there was more to this discrepancy than was at first apparent.

In the past decade, several papers have researched the question as to whether a lack of empathetic response is due to symptoms of autism or alexithymia, and recent research is indicating the possibility that alexithymia is more responsible for this than autism. I believe this could have far-reaching consequences for how we evaluate and treat individuals who are on the spectrum.

What is the research telling us?

A paper published in 2010 sought to measure empathetic response to another's physical pain by using functional magnetic resonance imaging (fMRI) (Bird *et al.* 2010). An fMRI scan measures brain activity by revealing any changes in blood flow and oxygenation.

The researchers used two groups of participants: a group of individuals diagnosed with high-functioning autism and a group of controls who were identified as neurotypical. All participants were required to bring a partner or a person close to them for the experiment. All individuals were initially measured for alexithymia.

By measuring brain activity, the researchers measured responses in brain activity in their participants when their partners were in physical pain. The findings showed that the degree of empathetic responses was the same for both the autistic and control group, but the level of response was dependent on the severity of alexithymia the participants were affected by and not whether they were on the autism spectrum.

In a later paper, Bird and Cook (2013) investigated the possibility as to whether it was the presence of alexithymia rather than traits of autism that were responsible for emotional impairments, reduced empathy and difficulty in recognizing another's emotions. The findings from this research provided further evidence that lack of empathy and recognizing emotions was 'due to the substantially elevated incidence of severe alexithymia present in the autistic population, and not autism *per se*' (Bird and Cook 2013, pp.5–6).

Further evidence continues to accrue. In 2016, a research paper presented by Shah and colleagues found that the capacity to read and interpret internal states was due to alexithymia rather than autism. More recently, exploration of the relationship between alexithymia and autism is beginning to highlight evidence that 'alexithymia is both a cause and consequence of autistic behaviours' (Poquérusse *et al.* 2018, p.1).

What are the implications of the research?

The implications of the research are far reaching as it could infer that the present criteria used to diagnose the milder end of autism could be misleading. If some of the criteria used is not due to an autistic trait but rather a consequence of being alexithymic, then this could result in some individuals on the spectrum not affected by alexithymia going unrecognized.

It also changes the present thinking that lack of empathy, an inability to recognize and verbalize introspective states and emotions and the capacity to recognize and respond acutely to the feelings and emotions in others are directly linked to autism. I have encountered many AS individuals who can discuss their feelings and interpret their internal states, and equally individuals who when another's feelings are explained in a logical and clear way can show empathy.

Another and very important implication of this research is its significance for therapy and treatment.

Therapy and treatment

I have found that therapies such as cognitive behavioural therapy (CBT) can be effective in treating alexithymia, and research supports this. Training could be offered to individuals with alexithymia to improve their ability to recognize emotional facial expressions (Cook *et al.* 2013). More recently, the benefits of mindfulness are being recognized, particularly in heightening awareness of internal sensations and their meanings (Gaigg, Cornell and Bird, 2018).

Being put under pressure to express feelings can be almost painful for the AS partner, and the more pressure that is exerted, the more they are likely to withdraw and say nothing at all. If this pattern of behaviour continues to go unrecognized, acknowledged or resolved, it can have a detrimental effect on both the partners and their relationship. Not being proffered any verbal expression of love and devotion can leave the NT partner feeling totally unloved and uncared for, often concluding that 'My AS partner cannot love me because, if they did, they would tell me how they feel about me.'

In a similar way, the AS partner, when asked how they feel, will often respond by saying that they are okay or fine. It appears that finding the correct expression to describe accurately how they feel is too difficult and overwhelming, hence the AS partner will not even attempt to say that in fact they are quite sad, frustrated or anxious. This is counterproductive as the AS partner can be left feeling unacknowledged and still trying to cope with the issues that are bothering them, while the NT partner may either just presume that everything is okay or, more likely, that everything is not okay and assume their partner is not confiding in them or is hiding something. The result of this will be that the NT partner might keep asking what is wrong, resulting in further withdrawal by the AS partner.

Any medium which avoids having to verbalize feelings will reduce stress and anxiety in the majority of individuals on the spectrum – this could be through music, art, colours or numbers, to mention a few.

Feelings in colour

The idea of colours symbolically representing feelings has been around for some time. I developed a way of replacing feelings with a colour, making this work for couples and families affected by autism. It is a technique I teach to the clients and professionals in my workshops. Its success is high as its simplicity makes it easily applicable to most situations, for all family members to use. Just the couple can use it or the whole family can be involved. I have found it works just as well with children as it does with adults. It can be developed with a therapist or it can be put together in the privacy of your home. Whichever is chosen, it can be fun putting it together and putting it to use.

When I put a colour chart together for a couple, it is important that they choose the expressions and colours which work for them as the chart must have meaning for them when they are using it. They will both be able to apply it to the other to discover what is happening for each of them. A colour chart allows for both creativity and imagination. For example, I might suggest having two colours for anger such as red and orange, where red can mean 'angry with you' and orange can mean 'angry with something else'. Many AS partners have discussed the difficulty they have in figuring out why their partner appears angry. They often assume it is because of something they have done. This will cause stress and may lead to shut down or withdrawal at a time when their partner may need them to talk or share a hug. If the AS partner is able to ask the colour their NT partner feels, the reply, if orange for example, will tell the AS partner that their partner's anger is about something else and not anything they have done, consequently reducing any anxiety or stress that may have been building up.

Another category I encourage is a colour for needing space – this is often white. For the AS family member, stressful situations can build up, especially at work, university or, for younger family members, school, where there can be a collection of stressful moments throughout the day. The AS individual will be working hard to keep pace with communication, figuring out what to say and how to say it – all stressors that can lead to a meltdown. Having space at the end of a busy day, having a quiet time simply to catch up and process what has gone on, can be vital to preserve well-being. Thirty minutes or an hour out to listen to music or to participate in their special interest will allow them this space. In the longer term, all will benefit as the AS individual will find it far easier to communicate and interact. Having this time to destress and process will be of real benefit to the AS individual. Sometimes, though, the AS partner will feel guilty about saying 'I want to be alone' or 'Please do not talk to me for an hour', especially when just home from work, having not seen their NT partner all day. Being able to say 'I feel white' should reduce any feelings of rejection as their partner then knows this is not about them and in a very short time life should be back to normal.

The Feelings in Colour Chart below is a very useful tool for couples and families. Coloured postcards are available from many craft shops, which could be bought, cut to an appropriate size and used by partners or family. It is a great way of working with children and adolescents who can arrive home feeling upset or frustrated about the day's events but feel unable to express those feelings to their parents in words.

Adding numbers

An essential addition to using colours as a method to describe feelings is to add a numerical value to those colours. It is not always enough to know that a person is red (angry) or black (depressed) as they could be slightly angry or very depressed. To ask the AS partner how angry or depressed they are may lead to further anger or depression as they may struggle to describe this in words. This is even more relevant if the AS individual is affected by alexithymia too. This question can cause frustration and the wrong reaction, leaving the NT partner feeling hurt that their attempt at showing care or concern for their partner's feelings has been rejected, making things worse between them.

The use of numbers can alleviate this. Once again, it is simple to use and easy to apply; it works in any given situation, whether private or public. Words to describe feelings can be abstract or perceptual in meaning. Words are often not definitive enough for AS partners. It is easier for them to make sense of feelings if they can do so by applying logic and making them finite.

This is how colours and numbers work together. If I ask a client with autism to imagine what colour anger would be, the answer is often red. I ask if they can picture this colour in their mind, or I will give them a red card to look at. Following this I use a number chart from one to ten and ask, 'Okay, if ten is the deepest red and one is the faintest red, what number red are you today?' Their answer will tell me immediately how angry they feel as numbers are often tangible for them.

The example shows a chart that I filled in with a young man I was working with. For him, black meant suicidal thoughts. On entering the counselling room, although he outwardly appeared to be okay, I asked him what colour he was, to which he replied black. I asked him how black and he answered eleven-and-a-half! In that reply, I knew that this was urgent and in need of immediate attention. I could have wasted a whole hour trying to encourage my client to tell me what was going on for him to no avail. I call this method a cognitive shortcut.

WORKSHEET

The Feelings in Colour Chart of Peter

Angry at you. . . . .   **Red**

Angry at someone else. . . . .   **Orange**

Sad/down/suicidal . . . .   **Black**

Happy. . . . .   **Yellow**

Confused. . . . .   **Green**

Needing space. . . . .   **White**

Feeling criticized. . . . .   **Purple**

Need a hug . . . .   **Pink**

Feeling rejected. . . . .   **Grey**

1   2   3   4   5   6   7   8   9   10

For couples and families, a colour for love is a useful addition. The importance of expressing love can often be overlooked in a couple's busy life. Sometimes the AS partner will just assume their partner knows they are loved, if only because of the things they do for them or because they told them a year ago or when they first met. Being told they are loved is emotional food for the NT partner. The more this is expressed, the happier and more secure the NT partner will feel. With the couples I work with, this is a topic that comes up very often. I may ask the AS partner, 'Do you love your partner?', to which they invariably answer, 'Yes.' I then ask, 'Do you tell your partner you love them?', to which they usually answer, 'They already know I do.' By enquiring further, it is usually the case that the AS partner finds the words difficult or the words they do find feel false. Additionally, having said the words, when pressed with 'How much?', the reply might be 'I do not know' or 'I am not sure' – not very flattering or reassuring for the NT partner. The AS partner who is able to say 'I am feeling pink (love)' and when asked 'How much?' can say 'Six' or 'Nine' will be on surer ground, thus leaving the NT partner reassured that they are loved. However, I would not recommend to ask questions about love when either partner is feeling angry, frustrated or stressed. At these times, feelings of love will not be a priority.

Using more than one colour at a time is similar to feeling more than one emotion at a time. Someone might be feeling criticized and sad, or they may feel happy and excited. I have worked with clients who went into great detail, using their colours and numbers to express how they felt. For example, asking what colour my client is today may elicit the following: 'I am a two for brown (anxious), green (confused) is seven and yellow is one (happy).' Some clients will use percentages, while others will enjoy using descriptions such as 'black with green streaks', or 'yellow with a grey outline'.

This method is versatile and adaptive and can be tailored to suit the person using it. It will not work for everyone, but for those it does work for it makes problems with emotional expression a thing of the past.

▬ Instructions for using the Feelings in Colour Chart

1. Have a selection of coloured crayons using as many colours as possible.

2. Think about an emotion most likely to come up for you, e.g. anger.

3. Enter the emotion on the line before the box.

4. Choose a colour that is representative of this emotion. If you are using the Feelings in Colour Chart as a family, then choose the colours between you.

5. Use this colour to fill in the box that links to the emotion.

6. Repeat steps 2–5 until as many boxes as required are filled in. If more are needed, use a new sheet.

7. Make copies of these so that all relevant people can make use of them.

8. Use the colour chart and numbers together to gain a deeper and quicker insight into how the person is feeling.

WORKSHEET

The Feelings in Colour Chart of . . . .

. . . .

. . . .

. . . .

. . . .

. . . .

. . . .

. . . .

. . . .

. . . .

1   2   3   4   5   6   7   8   9   10

Good communication and emotional expression are crucial for a relationship to run smoothly. As NT and AS partners talk different languages, it is inevitable that both these may frequently break down between them. A couple need to accept that there is a language difference and work hard at learning how to get it right. Being different does not make either partner wrong. As I described in Chapter 2, both are simply transmitting and receiving on a different wavelength.

Through practice, understanding will improve as each partner adjusts to the other's language. It is more likely that the NT partner will be adjusting the most, primarily due to their developed theory of mind allowing them to imagine another's situation. A person blind from birth would find it very difficult to imagine the colour blue, whereas a sighted person does not need to see blue to imagine what the colour blue looks like. It is therefore easier for a person who has the benefit of a high level of emotional intelligence and theory of mind to imagine the difficulty not having these skills may bring, in particular the difficulty the AS partner will have in reading non-verbal communication.

• Chapter 4 •

NON-VERBAL COMMUNICATION

THE misreading of non-verbal communication is responsible for many of the relational misunderstandings that occur between a couple. Non-verbal communication can be body language, nuance of intonation or physical touch. When describing the importance of non-verbal communication to couples, I outline that often the AS partner will have difficulty reading the NT partner's non-verbal communication. The AS partner may say, 'No one at work has difficulty communicating with me.' The NT partner may say, 'I seem to be the only person my partner cannot (or will not) read.' To the NT partner, the AS partner's difficulty in this area can appear to be selective or biased against them. There are reasons for this. It may also seem that problems have become worse the longer the relationship has gone on.

When we communicate with people we have recently met or we only know on a superficial level, we rely heavily on verbal communication, going into detail to explain what we mean. For example, communication at work is likely to be work related. It is highly probable that the AS partner will know exactly what is being discussed; they may even be an expert on the subject. This form of communication is far removed from the type shared by long-term intimate partners.

Over the course of time each partner will learn much about the other's ways – hence statements like:

- 'You know me inside out.'

- 'I only have to look at you and I know what you are thinking.'

- 'I am just being me – you know that.'

- 'How could you even think that after so long?'

- 'Surely you know me by now?'

The list is endless, but the one thing that all these statements suggest is that there is an assumption by one that the other can read their mind, so to speak, thus obviating the need to be explicit about what is actually going on in their own mind. These assumptions grow over the couple's time together and, particularly in an NT/AS relationship, these assumptions may develop into misunderstandings.

Assumptions

Being aware of these growing assumptions between them is very important for the couple. It is probably not something they have ever asked one another about. The AS partner will probably be quite unaware of the NT partner's nuance of body language in a given situation, while the NT partner will have presumed it has been understood. The AS partner's lack of or inappropriate response is likely to cause the NT partner to take it as a sign of not caring or of not being bothered on the part of their AS partner.

For example, the AS partner makes coffee for them both and they sit down to drink it together. Our NT partner gives the AS partner a tender look of 'thank you'. Her AS partner is not sure what the look meant and returns it with a blank stare. Both are now thinking something is wrong, and unless questions are asked they will part feeling negative.

With couples, I encourage the AS partner, whenever they find themselves feeling unsure about a look their partner has given them, to ask the NT partner what a look means or what they are thinking. I recommend that in response to this the NT partner might ask back, as shown in the illustration below, what their partner thought they were thinking. In this way, the couple can begin to discover what is really going on and not develop further misassumptions. This sounds simple but it can make such a difference. Checking that assumptions are correct or not can have a very positive effect on thoughts and feelings that may otherwise have been left in a negative state. Additionally, the AS partner may have stored the look their NT partner gave them and may recognize it more easily in the future.

It is not unusual for the AS partner to assume that the message they are picking up is negative. This may go back to childhood, especially if they were bullied as a child or misunderstood by others. They have come to expect negative reactions from others, and because their partner is such a relevant person in their lives this assumption of negativity can cause mayhem in the relationship and be very frustrating for the NT partner and very hurtful to the AS partner. The following case study provides an example of how this happens.

● CASE STUDY: KATHY AND ROGER

Kathy (aged 56) and Roger (aged 53) and they had been together for five years. Both suffered a painful divorce prior to their meeting. Their relationship had been quite volatile as both still harboured issues from the past. Kathy had been aware from the beginning that Roger was on the spectrum, and for the majority of the time Roger acknowledged this also.

For the past two months, Kathy had been asking Roger if he would cut the hedge. Roger hadn't done so and had recently been complaining of backache. Kathy was aware of this and sympathetic towards Roger as she knew all too well how painful backache could be.

Thinking that she was being helpful and taking the pressure off Roger, Kathy decided to do it herself. She was quite used to doing these type of jobs as she had lived alone for four years. However, when they moved in together, Roger had taken over the jobs in the garden and appeared to enjoy this role. On completing the hedge, Kathy was exhausted, but very proud that she had done such a good job. She was looking forward to seeing Roger's surprise when he came home from work.

The scenario went as follows.

Roger came in and, as always, took off his shoes, placed them on the shoe rack, put on his slippers, hung up his jacket, took off his tie and placed his keys on the hall shelf. He then gathered up his post and headed towards the kitchen to make a cup of tea.

Kathy was in the kitchen already boiling the kettle; the French doors were wide open showing an obvious view of the newly cut hedge.

'Hello Sweetie, have you had a good day?' Kathy enquired, looking very pleased with herself.

'Fine,' replied Roger, still evaluating his day and not yet having reached a conclusion as to whether it was bad or good.

'Shall we have our tea in the garden?' Kathy enquired with a big beam on her face as she walked out of the open doors with both cups of tea.

Roger did not reply but followed Kathy out into the garden. He did not reciprocate by asking Kathy what sort of day she had had and had not yet noticed the hedge.

'My day's been really busy,' Kathy prompted.

As this was a statement and not a question, Roger gave a simple 'Oh' in reply.

'Have you noticed?' Kathy enquired, looking at the hedge and not at Roger.

To this question, Roger found himself suddenly feeling defensive as he considered that sentence to be a trap that he felt he had been caught in many times in the past.

'Noticed what?' he said, his voice already irritated and becoming louder.

'The hedge! I did it all on my own!' Kathy beamed at him like a child wanting praise.

Roger did not read Kathy's look in this way. He interpreted it as triumphant sarcasm because he had not done the hedge and she was angry at him because she had had to do it herself. His voice was even louder as he reacted by saying, 'Why did you do that? Why didn't you ask me? You could have hurt yourself. I was going to do it. Why are you doing this, this is so unfair!'

This was not the reaction Kathy had expected, and the more she tried to explain, the worse it became, until Kathy also began to shout and say many things she did not mean.

Situations like this can have such a destructive effect on a relationship and leave both partners feeling horrible – but they can be avoided. Roger had completely misread Kathy's body language and facial expression, causing him to misinterpret her reasons for cutting the hedge. He was already angry with himself because his back problems were preventing him from fulfilling his usual roles in the home. He felt concern that Kathy could have hurt herself as the hedge was quite high and wrongly assumed that she was angry at him because he had not done it himself and consequently she had put herself at risk.

I often find with my clients that I need to explain in detail what was really going on for their partners. In this case, I would explain to Roger that Kathy was trying to please him by doing the hedge and she was quite competent at doing such jobs. She was concerned about his back, she was not trying to belittle him, but she wanted to make him proud of her and the fact she had managed it alone. Kathy equally needed to understand that without all the information required Roger was not able to read her intentions or her face and body language. In his previous marriage, his ex-wife had constantly belittled him and made negative comparisons between his abilities and her ex-husband's. The couple were able to learn from this experience and made some house rules for the future regarding household jobs.

It can be difficult for an NT individual to understand just how hard it is for someone on the spectrum to read another's face or body language, and I use an example to explain and help put this into context. I ask the NT partner to imagine they are living with someone who is partially blind, and ask the question as to whether they would expect that person to accurately read their facial expressions. Of course, the answer is no. People with AS could be described as very long sighted in this area and need as much added verbal information and clues as can be offered. Unfortunately, even verbal communications need to be checked due to difficulties in reading intonation.

Intonation of communication

When working with couples I constantly check out what has been heard, both by the couple from me and by each from the other. I do not assume that a message has been heard accurately and check whether a critical or negative message have been received when actually the opposite was meant. Not being able to read the intonation of a message can cause many misunderstandings. A single sentence can take on many different meanings according to how it is said. For instance, the following four sentences could be compliments:

- 'You *really* do make me laugh.'

- 'You *can* be so caring.'

- 'You *are* such a good listener.'

- 'Your *thoughtfulness* never ceases to amaze me.'

The italics are where the emphasis falls in the intonation but, in addition and difficult to convey here, it is how each sentence is spoken. Change the emphasis and the tone of each of the four sentences and they become critical, sarcastic or carry negative connotations:

- 'You really *do* make me laugh!'

- 'You can be *so* caring!'

- 'You are *such* a good listener!'

- 'Your thoughtfulness *never* ceases to amaze me!'

When the ability to interpret the difference between sarcasm, irony or a genuine statement is limited, it is not surprising that misunderstandings arise in communication. An AS partner may not be aware that this difficulty exists for them. They have probably never learned or acquired these subtleties of intonation. Often a negative or literal interpretation is taken when neither is intended. Learning about autism – how it affects an AS partner and how the differences between AS and NT can complicate non-verbal communication – is important. Below I have set out a way an NT partner can check out how well their AS partner is doing in understanding them. If the couple are both AS, then it will need a third party, possibly a therapist, to do this with you.

This test should be a fun thing for a couple to try out, so it is important that it is tried when both partners are feeling good and the relationship is reasonably stable. Remember, you're trying to learn about one another.

■ Instructions for using the Intonation Test

1. Each partner should have a worksheet.

2. The NT partner should read each statement to the AS partner, making a note on their sheet as to whether their intonation is giving a negative or positive message. Remember that each statement can mean different things depending on the intonation.

3. The AS partner should tick the box that they feel is how the statement is meant. For example, if the sentence sounds like sarcasm and therefore negative, then tick the negative box.

4. When the NT partner has read all the statements, work out together how well the AS partner has understood the statements. Try repeating the statements that were not understood correctly again so that the AS partner can perhaps hear the intonation.

AS Intonation Test

You make me laugh.

Positive ☐   Negative ☐

Well that was really clever.

Positive ☐   Negative ☐

Thank you for thinking of me.

Positive ☐   Negative ☐

No it's okay – I'll do it.

Positive ☐   Negative ☐

You just sit there and rest, my love.

Positive ☐   Negative ☐

Have you got a problem with that?

Positive ☐   Negative ☐

What did you say?

Positive ☐   Negative ☐

Are you okay to do that?

Positive ☐   Negative ☐

You really hit the jackpot with that one.

Positive ☐   Negative ☐

Where did you get that dress/shirt?

Positive ☐   Negative ☐

The more the NT partner understands how their partner's brain works and how their partner reads both them and others, the fewer misunderstandings there will be. Likewise, the AS partner has to appreciate that they do not always read a situation correctly, so when they do feel unsure or criticized about a look or something their partner has said, it is important that the AS partner asks.

Working on the non-verbal side of the relationship will not be easy if the AS partner is sensitive to perceived criticism and unable to ask their partner questions when they feel that they are being criticized. The NT partner is not likely to be aware that the AS partner has perceived something they said as critical. The NT partner should look out for these signs, such as a blank look, that might suggest misinterpretation and check it out with their partner.

In the coffee example, I encouraged our AS partner to ask the NT partner why they had looked at them in a certain way. However, maybe when our NT partner received a blank stare, they could have verbalized how they were feeling a little confused. It's about being aware of these signs and not letting them go by unchecked.

The AS partner will believe that if the NT partner says something, then that is what the NT partner means. It will not occur to the AS partner that there is a hidden meaning within the intonation. The Intonation Test should help the couple to appreciate how this happens.

How can this pattern be changed? If this has become a major concern and the couple finds it difficult to stop and ask, they may need to work this through with a therapist. Learning about this absence of non-verbal skills from a third party, especially if the relationship is struggling, may be received better by the AS partner. To identify what it is that has been misread will require the couple to pause the conversation, usually as soon as something appears to have been misunderstood. There may be that blank look on the AS partner's face, telling the NT partner that something may not have been understood correctly, or the AS partner may abruptly disengage and walk away. Whichever way it is, the NT partner is more likely to sense this and may even have witnessed it many times.

MAD moments

I call these moments when a misunderstanding has occurred MAD (Misread And Dodgy) moments. They need to be verbalized with one partner saying, 'I think this is a MAD moment.' The NT partner is likely to be best equipped to identify these moments and pause the conversation. When discussing the MAD moment that has occurred, communication should be clear and direct, with both taking their turn to speak, respecting one another's right to have their say. The following are a few rules I recommend using when a MAD moment is identified.

Rules for Misread And Dodgy (MAD) moments

- *IDENTIFICATION* (either partner): A look, a comment, an uncomfortable feeling, walking away.

- *PAUSE* (either partner): Achieved by saying, 'I think this is a MAD moment.'

- *SPEAKING UP* (AS): Saying what has been heard (without interruption).

- *EXPLAINING* (NT): Saying what was meant in what was said and the true meaning behind it.

- *UNDERSTANDING* (AS): Repeating back what has been explained and saying if it is now understood.

- *REPEATING* (NT): If necessary, stating again what was meant.

- *ACCEPTING* (both): Confirming that the true meaning is now understood and accepting that this was a MAD moment.

- *INTERRUPTING* (both): Not allowed by either at any time.

MAD moments can occur at any time, whether the couple are in private or public situations. MAD moments in public can be harder to prevent and rectify, so other strategies have to be put into place. Unfortunately, MAD moments are just one of the stressors that can lead to meltdown. Meltdowns will affect all AS individuals as they try to cope with managing a very socially and emotionally unpredictable world, and may be further hindered by sensory overload. Meltdowns can occur at the most unexpected time and in the most unlikely places, regardless of who is around at the time. This brings us to our next important chapter, 'Meltdowns'.

Chapter 5

MELTDOWNS

A FEW years ago, I attended a two-day conference for Oxford Autism. All the speakers there were excellent and included Professor Tony Attwood, Dr Michelle Garnett, Ann Memmott, Tilus Clark and the youngest member of the team, James Hoodless. James is a young man diagnosed with autism who works as an autism trainer. His talk focused on meltdowns, and his description of a meltdown was detailed and highly informative – in fact, it was one of the most honest and accurate accounts I have ever been privileged to listen to. James brought home the reality of living with meltdowns, the difficulty and embarrassment they cause the individual, and how, from his personal perspective, they could be avoided. James used an analogy of a dam in a river, and the water behind the dam represented emotions.

A meltdown, James depicted, is caused by the water building up higher and higher behind the dam until, without warning, the floodgates burst and all the water (emotions) comes gushing out. He continued to describe how it can be something quite small and trivial that can act as the trigger for a meltdown and yet be capable of producing the sensation of having a massive ball of internal panic developing inside. All focus will be on this one trigger which caused the panic, and for that time nothing and no one else will be relevant. James described how a meltdown has to run its course once it is triggered, and no amount of logical or rational communication will prevent it once it has reached this stage. He warned how at least 90 minutes must be allowed for a meltdown to subside, as trying to intervene before this time could cause the meltdown to flare up even more and start all over again.

James believed that for him the meltdown he described could have been avoided if the issues leading up to it had been communicated to someone who understood and could have helped. He also reminded the audience that autism is a communication difficulty, so this is not always an option that is acted on.

The excellent talk James offered at the conference was based on his own perspective, and not all individuals on the spectrum will experience and react to a meltdown in the same way as James did. However, meltdowns in one form or another will affect all individuals on the spectrum. Meltdowns can take three forms: fight, flight or freeze. These three reactions are known as the universal reaction to threat experienced by all individuals; however, in the case of autism, meltdowns can occur without any warning. This can be due to the AS individual having limited self-awareness of the crisis building up internally and/or an inability to resolve or communicate the reason for the stress and anxiety that are growing. Meltdowns can be highly reactive, and afterwards the AS individual may have little awareness of the negative effect their meltdown has had on those around them.

Regardless of whether the response to a meltdown is fight, flight or freeze, all forms of meltdown can have an impact on the couple relationship and can result in both partners feeling miserable and drained. However, of the three responses, it is the fight (reactive) response that can cause the most damage to the couple and family. The consequences of a reactive meltdown can be devastating for both partners and cause long-term suffering to the relationship. The majority of AS clients I have worked with have expressed that they will do or try anything to avoid a meltdown, particularly a reactive meltdown. My clients have described meltdowns as a feeling of being totally overwhelmed, confused, bewildered and unable to process thoughts or communicate in a way that is acceptable or rational. This internal conundrum of jumbled feelings and emotions can take over the individual and render them feeling useless, as they find themselves rapidly gushing through the floodgates of the overloaded dam, as described by James Hoodless.

At this point, you may be asking the question, well if it is that bad why can't AS individuals just find a way to not have them? The problem is that meltdowns are very difficult to predict, not just for the person on the spectrum but also for all those around them. A meltdown can appear to come out of nowhere, at the most unexpected times and places, and often over something very trivial. They are very similar to the English weather – difficult to predict – and even the most reliable weather forecaster is prone to getting it wrong!

While James Hoodless likened meltdowns to a bursting dam, others have used the analogy of a volcano erupting. I often use the analogy of a thunderstorm, the type that often appears to come out of nowhere, without warning. However, once the dynamics that create a thunderstorm are understood, they can sometimes be predicted – not prevented, only predicted.

Three basic ingredients are required to form a thunderstorm: moisture to produce the clouds and rain, unstable air and, finally, lift. Thunderstorms can happen at any time and almost anywhere.

The moisture that builds up could be likened to a build-up of stress. Often this build-up will have been accumulating for days or weeks. Some NT partners may have sensed a negative atmosphere in the relationship but not been able to figure out what was causing it. They describe how they have enquired from their AS partner as to whether they were alright or if anything was wrong and were frequently told that everything was fine. This can leave some NT partners doubting their own intuition or convincing themselves that it must be them who are creating the atmosphere.

The second ingredient required to trigger a thunderstorm is unstable air, and as little nuances and minor irritations creep into the relationship, it can begin to feel unstable and insecure. If this is not addressed or reduced then this build-up continues to the final stage, lift. In a relationship, lift is the breaking point that triggers the meltdown. Lift is produced by differences in air density that create an upward surge and it can be caused by something trivial or minor like a light breeze or something huge like a mountain. Whichever form the trigger takes, it will nearly always result in a storm which, like a meltdown, can have a habit of occurring at the most unexpected times.

All meltdowns are different – how quickly they progress, their severity and how quickly they pass will be different according to the situation and the individual experiencing it. Some warning signs, like the dark clouds that precede a thunderstorm, are more obvious, but sometimes meltdowns appear to come out of absolutely nowhere.

So, what can be done by either partner to avoid or lessen the way a meltdown occurs in this reactive way?

Using the analogy of the thunderstorm again, one would be looking out for the dark clouds, the spitting rain and a general oppressive atmosphere. It is this general atmosphere and feelings of tension in the air that most NT partners pick up on.

If an NT partner suspects that something is not quite right, it is important to follow these intuitive hunches because they are often right even though their partner might not agree with them. It is advised at these slightly ambivalent times that the NT partner does not pressurize their partner into acknowledging that there is something amiss as this could escalate the speed a meltdown is reached. The reason for this is that the AS partner, although aware something is amiss, may struggle with finding the words to express how they are feeling, especially if affected by alexithymia too. Always remember that emotional language uses up the AS partner's resources very quickly as it is something they can find very difficult. Another reason for the AS partner's lack of acknowledgement is the fear that their answer could trigger a confrontation with their partner, so they will not risk being open and admitting to their feelings.

The AS partner will be finding it increasingly difficult at this time to interpret their NT partner's body language or voice intonation. They will be expecting and perceiving negatives in neutral situations and communications.

For the NT partner, spotting the signs early is essential, and in the following list are some of the visual and behavioural signs that the NT partner might look out for. It is equally important for the AS partner to be aware of how their body and mind might be reacting to a build-up of stress, so it is a good idea for both to fill in the Stress Indicator List and then compare their observations together.

If you are the NT partner, take time to tick the stress indicators that you have noticed in your partner when they are becoming stressed. For example, if it has been noticed that the AS partner avoids eye contact prior to a meltdown, or they become more reactive than usual to sensory stimuli, tick the appropriate right-hand box. If you are the AS partner then tick the stress indicators that you are aware affect you. If there are other indicators not mentioned in the list that either of you are aware of, use the blank rows to enter them. After completion, share your observations with your partner and, if possible, discuss these together.

■ Instructions for completing the Stress Indicator List

1. Choose a time when you are both calm and relaxed.

2. Try to be sure you will not be disturbed.

3. Have a separate copy each to fill in.

4. The NT partner – tick the stress indicators you have observed.

5. The AS partner – tick the stress indicators you are aware that you do.

6. Add any you are aware of that are not listed.

7. Share your lists together and discuss the contents.

WORKSHEET
The Stress Indicator List

STRESS INDICATORS	TICK
Changes in body language and behaviour	
Avoiding eye contact	
Flickering eyelids	
Facial tics	
Tapping fingers	
Twirling wedding (or other) rings	
Fiddling with hair	
Rigid body language	
Rapid/faster body movements	
Taking longer to reply to questions	
Sharpness in voice and movements	
Rocking movements	
Covering ears	
Turning music up loud	
Irritability/low tolerance towards external factors	
Sound of others:	
Chewing	
Crunching	
Swallowing	
Television/radio	
Clock ticking	

Partner's voice	
Children laughing, shouting, playing	
Background noise (lawn mowers, fridges, fans, dogs barking)	
Over reaction to tastes or smells	
Lights	

It is useful to use this list to help familiarize and become aware of the warning signs that will alert you to ask your partner what number they are on the Stress Self-Assessment Scale (SSAS) (this will be discussed and explained later in this chapter). Unfortunately, by the time these signs are noticed, it might be too late to discuss what is wrong. If communication appears to be a no-go area and changing the topic to something the AS partner would find interesting has not worked, then maybe it is worth trying time apart. It could be arranged beforehand that if the AS partner reaches a specific number on the SSAS then they will take themselves off somewhere and try to destress, perhaps by going for a walk or listening to music. However, if this is not happening, then it may be up to the NT partner to leave the situation. Time apart can be beneficial for the NT partner to enable alone time for self-care, hobbies, mindfulness or exercise. It is important not to allow the negative atmosphere to have an impact on their self-esteem or mood.

Fight, flight or freeze response – different forms of meltdowns

The majority of the AS clients I have worked with will do anything to avoid a meltdown and loss of control. Meltdowns are exhausting because of the energy they use up. All my AS clients experience meltdowns differently but they are all a consequence of a build-up of stress and then overload. I have found that although the fight response does occur for some of my clients, most would rather implode than explode. This is due to their extreme fear of any type of confrontation and they will actively do anything to avoid this, whether it means running away from the situation or completely shutting down and not communicating. This response is known as flight or freeze, which is quite different, and a passive response compared to a reactive fight response.

The fight, flight or freeze reactions to meltdowns are discussed in detail below. It can be helpful for both partners to be aware and recognize what type of meltdown affects them most. Although all types of meltdown responses are difficult to manage when they occur, they can present in very different ways and levels of external severity. I use the word external because although the external reactions of a meltdown can vary greatly between individuals, the internal turmoil the individual experiences is the same. I will start with the most detrimental to the relationship, which is known as the fight response.

Fight response

This is the most destructive of the three reactions and the one that will require the most time and effort to change. The definition of fight used for this chapter includes shouting, using offensive language, slamming doors and stamping feet. It does not include threatening physical behaviour, physical violence, damage to property or severe anger outbursts in front of the children. If a partner exhibits any of these then it is nothing to do with having mild autism but because of the person they are, and no individual should tolerate living in a relationship where they or their children are scared, threatened, being hurt or having their possessions damaged. This applies regardless of whether it is the AS or NT partner who is displaying violent or aggressive behaviour, and regardless of their gender or sexuality.

The fight reaction comes under two different categories according to the individual's basic personality.

THE DENIER

The first and the most damaging to the relationship is what I call the denier. The denier is an AS individual who has not accepted they might be on the spectrum and has not sought to find out whether they are. They are often unwilling to accept any responsibility for their behaviour or the effect/consequences of their actions. When this individual goes into the fight reaction, it can be very damaging and is often directed strongly towards their partner. This damage is further prolonged by their total denial afterwards of any blame or responsibility for what occurred. Unfortunately, the denier will blame their partner or family member for everything that occurred, including their own reaction to it.

Fortunately, this group is in the minority and it is their basic personality, not autism, that causes this reaction. These individuals in denial are the most difficult to live with. The NT partner is living with someone affected by a condition which is neither acknowledged or diagnosed and even the suggestion of autism is met with total denial. Unfortunately, if someone is in total denial of their own shortfalls and communication difficulties, then it is highly probable that they will blame their partner for the issues that are reoccurring in the relationship. This will mean that resolving issues will be impossible. Change for this group is extremely difficult and I have only seen change occur when an acceptance or a diagnosis of autism transpires.

THE APOLOGIZER

The apologizer is the remorseful response. The AS partner will acknowledge *in time* the part they played in the meltdown, and its effect. Unfortunately, it can often take much time, patience and determination by the NT partner to explain in a clear and logical way before these apologies happen. However, although there may eventually be many apologies and signs of remorsefulness, the AS partner may still not be too sure what they are apologizing for. It will be their drive to restore equilibrium in the relationship and return to a place of security and calm that will motivate them to apologize profusely, often promising it will not happen again.

Flight response

Flight is a far better alternative to fight and can have less impact on those around the individual; however, it can still come as a great surprise and sometimes be very inconvenient. Flight is like imploding rather than exploding; the energy surge that meltdown causes travels inwards rather than being directed outwards, often at someone else. Unfortunately, the flight response involves just that – flight! This can mean leaving the room/house/restaurant/venue/local area/town/city or, in extreme cases, the country! This could be via any form of transport or mode available, including simply legging it to the nearest bus stop! Flight can last anything from a few hours to a few days! This can cause major concern for those who care for the person especially if their partner turns their mobile off and does not make contact.

I do recommend to NT partners that if they are with an individual who goes into the flight response it is wise to let them do just that and to not block their exit or try to make them discuss the issue in the present moment. To do this can provoke a fight response, which, although out of character, can occur if the individual feels trapped.

Freeze response

So many of my AS clients hate confrontation and will do anything to avoid it, so when overload occurs, they will completely shut down, almost like turning off a computer or a light – everything is switched off. All feelings will be shut out in order to maintain control. The freeze response is similar to the flight response but minus the running away, as often circumstances do not permit leaving. Freeze is like the rabbit caught in the headlights and, just like the other two responses, is a form of survival. As with flight, communication will cease, eye contact is avoided and there will be a complete refusal to discuss or debate the topic in question at the time. The individual may go and work on their computer, listen to music or totally focus on a task to try and manage the stress and anxiety they are dealing with.

I recommend that the NT partner allows this to follow its natural course in the knowledge that their partner's brain is slowly processing and making sense of what is going on for them. Be patient and wait, as to try to initiate a discussion at this time or to prevent the opportunity for space and time the AS partner needs will only provoke a more volatile response or cause their partner to turn to flight or fight.

In whatever form it takes, overload leading to meltdown is not a nice place to be for either partner. For the AS partner, it is a loss of control when adrenaline takes over the mind and the body and causes havoc for all concerned. For the NT partner, it is frustrating, lonely and can often feel very hurtful.

No one wants to be at odds with their partner and most will wish to restore the equilibrium in the relationship. However, resolution can be hindered by the ability to recall accurately the events that occurred.

Selective memory

Trying to resolve issues after a meltdown is frequently hindered by what can appear to be an episode of memory loss by the AS partner and they may struggle to recall both the order of events and what was said. The biology to this is that when in fight, flight or freeze, the frontal lobe and hippocampus in the brain shut down, affecting memory function.

It can make it very difficult to resolve an issue when the memory of events recorded is very different for each partner. With regards to the emotional content of the issues that occurred, it is likely that the NT partner's record of events is more reliable. AS individuals are excellent at recalling logical and factual information, but emotional information can become lost in translation.

It can take a lot of trust on behalf of the AS partner to accept and believe that they really did and said what their NT partner is telling them and that it was as bad as their partner is saying it was. If a more accurate record of events can be established then there is far better chance that the issue can be resolved. Sometimes though, if the issue is too painful to be discussed, then maybe having a third party present, such as in couple therapy, could be a way forward.

The fight response in any form is difficult to live with and a lot of my work in therapy is to help AS individuals change the fight response to flight. Meltdowns cannot be avoided but how they are expressed can be adapted if the AS individual wants to change this and make improvements to their relationship. Fight can be changed to flight.

Changing fight to flight

If an AS individual is prone to go into the fight response and they are not in denial about this, they will be aware of the damage it causes, both to how they feel about themselves and to those around them that they care about. This is a topic that often comes up in the therapy room as the AS partner is aware that, in some cases, if they do not change, they could risk losing their partner, family and friends.

One of the ways I work on helping the AS individual change from fight to flight is to explain to them, as in this book, exactly what is happening in their brain that causes the meltdown. AS individuals are very logical thinkers and I refer to the description I use in Chapter 1, 'A different way of thought processing'. I find that if an individual on the spectrum has a complete understanding of a concept and it makes logical sense to them, then change is more likely to occur. So, understanding how the effects of stress, sensory overload and adrenaline all lead up to a fight response can make a huge difference to how a meltdown is perceived and handled. Knowledge and understanding will increase the capacity to control how the meltdown presents itself. Using techniques such as distraction and mindfulness has helped many individuals on the spectrum to gain control and reduce the build-up of stress, all of which can help change the response from fight to flight. Before I move on to suggesting techniques that can be used to help gain control over emotions, I want to explore the frequently avoided topic of the NT partner and meltdowns.

What about the NT partner and meltdowns?

It is not always the AS partner who is prone to meltdowns; the NT partner can equally be affected by an overreaction to stress. It is less likely they will occur in a public place or in front of family and friends, but nevertheless in private they can equally reach a point of not being able to manage or control the pent-up feelings of frustration, anger and desperation they may be carrying inside.

I have listened to NT partners shamefully recount episodes where they have reacted in a very hostile and volatile way towards their partner, in particular if the NT partner is female. Many have been saddened and deeply regretful that they reached such a point of no control. They feel as if they behaved and spoke in a way that is totally out of character for them and have shamefully acknowledged that they said some very cruel words and behaved in an aggressive way.

Frequently, this reaction is born out of frustration of not being able to communicate their feelings or have them reciprocated or understood by their AS partner. It seems no matter how hard they try their partner never quite 'gets it'. This feeling may have been building up for a long time and the NT partner will often have tried to find many ways to explain their frustration and attempt to get their emotional needs met. They may have tried showing their AS partner much empathy and care in the hope their partner would learn to reciprocate their feelings.

When the NT partner fails to get their emotional needs met, caring and sympathy can turn into anger and frustration, which unfortunately exacerbates the issues between the couple. The AS partner will be acutely tuned in to any display of anger from their partner and will instantly back off and withdraw emotionally and often physically for fear that a confrontation is about to ensue. Unfortunately, this will increase the NT partner's feelings of frustration for having their emotional needs remain unmet. The NT partner will become more needy and angry and the AS partner will become more distant and withdrawn…until the NT partner cannot control their pent-up feelings of frustration any longer. Whether or not anger outbursts are coming from the NT or AS partner, aggressive/violent or threatening behaviour towards a partner is never acceptable and it is important that help is sought by one or both partners to address this, if it occurs.

Not all forms of anger are abusive or threatening. Anger should be a healthy, natural emotion with the function of protecting us from perceived threat. Anger can also be a secondary emotion used to cover up a number of primary feelings such as hurt or embarrassment. Hence it is not the anger that is the problem but how the anger is managed and how it is communicated or not. Anger left to build up to high levels can lead to explosive outbursts that can be hurtful to both parties. It is important for the NT partner to explore and recognize the cause of their anger towards their partner so as to address the issues and unmet needs that lie beneath their anger. It is also important that ways are learned to manage anger so that its impact is not hurtful to them or their partner. One way is to put into place some rules regarding anger and arguing.

Three rules for good arguing

I suggest couples follow three very important rules for good arguing. If these are followed, arguing can become a healthy debate in which both can share their different perspectives without the fear of confrontation.

- First rule: No physical abuse.

- Second rule: No verbal abuse.

- Third rule: No bringing up the past.

First rule: No physical abuse

Physical abuse should not be tolerated in any relationship. Just because a couple are an NT and AS combination does not make this maxim less so. Physical abuse breaks all the rules that govern respect for the safety and well-being of the other person during a discussion or argument. It rips apart the very core of the relationship and leaves it feeling controlled, under threat and intimidating.

In my research (Aston 2003a), I found that the majority of AS partners would rather stay in a dysfunctional relationship in which they were being abused than leave it and live alone, partly due to fear of change and partly due to the dependency that can develop on the NT partner. However, the NT partner may stay in the relationship in which they are being abused because they live in hope that their partner will change.

Second rule: No verbal abuse

Verbal abuse is a form of control by one person towards another. The verbally abused person is stripped of their self-worth, self-esteem and confidence in their abilities. Verbal abuse can be painful and destructive and have long-term psychological effects. Using sarcasm, double meanings, name calling, threats or humour at the expense of another are forms of verbal abuse and should be avoided at all times. Shouting, stamping of feet or slamming of doors are forms of verbal abuse, as these are audible expressions designed to intimidate and control.

Third rule: No bringing up the past

Bringing up issues from the past is often used to make the other partner feel guilty. This is unfair as neither partner can change what has already happened. The best either partner can ever do is learn from their experiences and try to do things differently in the future.

Unfortunately, due to the frequent breakdown of communication between AS and NT partners, there may be many unresolved issues. This could be due to a belief that the other partner will not understand or get the point, or either partner fears that the raising of issues will make things worse. Consequently, issues get stored up. I call this 'pebbles in the bucket', as with each unresolved issue each partner adds a pebble to their bucket. When an argument ensues, they turn to their respective buckets and proceed to throw the pebbles (metaphorically) at one another.

Strategies to avoid breaking the three rules

The difficulty is in realizing that a point has been reached where a breach of the rules is about to occur. For example, a couple may be discussing an issue where one partner is doing most of the talking and dominating the discussion. The other partner is sat quietly, saying little, even with a benign expression, and there are no outward indications that they are becoming either frustrated or angry. How does either know they need to pause before this explodes into verbal or physical abuse? One way is the Feelings in Colour Chart that I have already explained (see Chapter 3) where the AS partner can have an accurate method of expression by using the numbers to express the extent of their frustration or anger. However, if this does not work and relating to colours proves difficult, then it may help to visualize an active object and relate it to the build-up of feeling the AS person is experiencing. For some this can be a pressure cooker. In this instance, I have used the frustration or anger thermometer, as suggested by Tony Attwood in his highly informative book *Asperger's Syndrome: A Guide for Parents and Professionals* (1998). The anger thermometer, as its name suggests, is more applicable to situations that are building up to danger point.

The frustration or anger thermometer

I ask clients to visualize a thermometer, or better still I show them a picture of a thermometer. I ask them to try and picture the red liquid rising as the temperature rises, suggesting they think of their frustration or anger as a rising temperature on a scale of one to ten. How high does their thermometer have to go before control is lost? Six? Seven? By keeping this number in mind, the AS partner can convey to their partner that their level of frustration or anger is reaching danger point, whereupon preventative measures can be implemented to calm the situation.

Taking the example above of the couple who are having the one-sided discussion, the partner who is doing most of the talking could stop and ask their partner what number their thermometer has reached. Conversely, the partner staying quiet but feeling frustrated or angry could simply interject with 'My thermometer is at seven', thus informing the other that it's time to pause.

This use of the thermometer works for both NT and AS partners, so long as they have agreed that as soon as the other partner indicates their boiling point is approaching, they break off and apply a calming strategy. These calming strategies will be different for different people. For example, many of the adolescents I work with find music very therapeutic. Music can be mood altering and some AS people are highly tuned in to rhythmic sound. If seven is the recognized level that can be reached on the thermometer while still maintaining control, when that point is reached, allowing the AS person to step back and plug into their iPod or MP3 player, for example, will potentially reduce the frustration or anger, avoiding breaking the good arguing rules.

For others, the calming strategy might be to use deep-breathing techniques, to find a quiet place to sit, or to become absorbed in a special interest. Once again, it is trial and error in finding what works for each individual. Couples and families need to find out what works best for the AS person in order to allow them to apply the calming strategies that work.

Although I talk about the AS partner here, these techniques work equally well for the NT partner when faced with the possibility of an eruption into abusive behaviour. The NT partner may overreact in a subliminal attempt to start an argument – an argument that will allow unresolved issues to be aired. Many NT partners find it difficult to get their AS partner to talk. This subconscious reaction is often due to the weight of their 'bucket of pebbles'. Arguments and discussions are healthy so long as the three rules are not broken. It is difficult, at times, to take a deep breath and remember not to break the three rules. The thermometer can be applied whenever any of the three rules are in danger of being broken and when there is a sense that stress between the couple is building up.

Unresolved issues

I mentioned earlier the 'pebbles in a bucket' each partner may be carrying around, ready to throw at each other when a disagreement occurs. The best way of preventing a store of unresolved issues from accumulating, or a collection of negative distorted memories from developing, is to resolve the issues when they happen or shortly afterwards. The use of the colour chart, thermometer or applying whole sentences to avoid misunderstandings may work. Sometimes though, if issues remain undiscussed and allowed to fester for too long, they can reach a point that becomes overwhelming and will feel unsurmountable.

Dealing with unresolved issues is best timed for when the couple are not angry or at loggerheads with each other. This can feel difficult for both, as when they are getting on well it can seem destructive to risk bringing up an issue that may destroy the harmony. This is why unresolved issues are often only raised when the couple have already fallen out, so taking the risk of bringing up even more issues is of no consequence.

Keeping to the analogy of pebbles in the bucket, I have worked with couples to make this analogy real. I recommend they each buy a bucket, not too big, maybe a child's sandcastle bucket. When an issue comes up that bothers them and is unresolved, they should write it down briefly on a post-it note or piece of paper and put it in their bucket.

When the timing feels right and the couple have time and are not stressed, they should take just one unresolved issue out of each bucket and discuss it together or bring it to discuss with a therapist.

Unresolved issues can be easier to write down than to say. The written word is easier for the AS partner to deliberate on and process. Having a sheet made for this purpose is useful. The following is an example of how it could be laid out. Always remember to stick to only one issue at a time. If an issue has become too sensitive to bring up or work out together, it may be an idea to take that issue to therapy where it can be approached in the safety of the therapy room.

▬ Instructions for using the Unresolved Issues worksheets

1. Decide what is the most important issue for you to be resolved.
2. Agree together beforehand that having a different perception of an issue does not make either perception wrong.
3. Try not to use the 'you' word. Use 'I' whenever possible.
4. Ensure that the reply date or time is realistic.
5. The AS partner often needs more time to think things through, so it might take a little longer.
6. The focus should be on resolution, not provocation, and should not lead to further disagreements.

WORKSHEET
Unresolved Issues

....
....
....
....
....
....
....
....
....
....
....
....
....
....
....

WORKSHEET
Unresolved Issues Reply

....
....
....
....
....
....
....
....
....
....
....
....
....
....
....
....

Strategies for avoiding meltdowns

As well as applying the worksheets in this book there are many ways to reduce, divert or convert the energy that causes anger into more positive directions. There are many mindfulness and relaxation techniques that can help both partners in the relationship to stay in control and find a sense of calm. Below is a simple exercise I have developed for both to try; it is all about controlled breathing and focus. As soon as either partner recognizes that they are becoming overstressed or confused or feel unable to cope, then just stop for a few minutes and work through the next worksheet.

The Be Still Technique (for both partners)

Be aware of the speed your thoughts are racing through your mind – if possible, shut your eyes – and imagine a steam train racing along the tracks. In your imagination, slowly pull back the brake lever. Imagine the wheels slowly grinding to a halt, imagine the noise as the engine slowly comes to a standstill at the station. There is a bench on the platform, the station is empty. Step down from the driver's carriage and sit on the bench. Lean back, relax, breathe in deeply.

Self-Talk – Tell your mind to be still, to be calm and to slow down. If possible, close your eyes.

Introspection – Be aware of the tension in your body: your face, neck, shoulders; your arms, hands, fingers; your chest, hips, stomach; your legs, feet, toes.

Loosen your muscles, especially in your face, relax your mouth, relax your jaw, let your shoulders fall down and arms hang loosely at your side; place your hands on your lap if you prefer.

Listen to your breathing…in and out…in and out…slowly, rhythmically, controlled, feel the stillness in your mind, calm, still…and at peace.

When you are ready, you can get back on to your train or you can just stay where you are, enjoying the solitude of the empty platform.

Physical exercise

Physical exercise has proved very beneficial to many AS individuals and it doesn't matter what form it takes. For some it is a brisk walk around the block, for others it might mean calling into their leisure/sports centre on the way home and having a workout in the gym or a swim in the pool, followed by a relax in the sauna or steam room. Eradicating the pent-up stress from the body and clearing the mind is a first-class way of aiding the transition from work to home. Everyone will benefit from this as the AS partner will be more ready to join in with home life, feeling energized and free from the stressors of the busy day.

Open/wild/cold water swimming

I am receiving more and more very positive reports from AS individuals regarding the benefits of open water swimming and in particular cold water swimming. Some feel that it has absolutely turned their lives around, especially if this becomes a special interest. In addition to the psychological boost it provides, open water swimming can also increase self-esteem and confidence and provide a fantastic network of supportive and encouraging swimmer friends. Below is an account sent to me by an AS adult:

> As a person who overthinks and worries needlessly when in a state of anxiety, I have constantly tried ways to distract my thought processes from this pattern. I have tried many ways, usually unsuccessfully.
>
> Then I discovered open water swimming. Now I can put myself into an unknown where all my thoughts are needed to be in the moment. This is called cross-adaption. I found that my whole self was totally engulfed and occupied physically and mentally. I was totally focused to the exclusion of everything else. Perfect for an Aspie as this is our strength. I later went on to enjoy cold water swimming. There is wide support that the effects of depression and other mental health issues can be greatly reduced or in some cases eliminated completely.

Music

Another way that has been found to prevent or defuse a meltdown is to use music. Having an accessible playlist of soothing and feel good music on an iPod, mobile phone or a computer can work wonders. Music and autism appear to have some very strong links in a therapeutic way, and the sound of music can help to block out intrusive thoughts. The autistic brain rarely switches off or shuts down and can constantly regurgitate and replay conversations. The problem is that it will be the negatives that keep getting played. Music can act as a barrier to shut out these intrusive, negative thoughts and replace them with uplifting and calming melodies.

Exercise for the AS partner

Take time to select and compile a list of music you find relaxing, calming and uplifting. If you are in surroundings that prevent you from playing your music out loud, such as travelling on the Underground, then use headphones. If you have Bluetooth in your car, you could play your music while driving to work or on your way home to help you destress.

Using numbers

Using numbers has helped many couples and is a coping strategy I have used in counselling for years, putting together with a client what I call a Stress Self-Assessment Scale (SSAS). This is a very quick and easy way of finding out exactly what level of stress the AS partner is experiencing and for them to have a way to convey how they feel to another. This scale needs to be completed by the AS partner at a time when they are not stressed. The scale should be shared with their partner and any other important family members, so they know what the relevant numbers mean. The scale will also help the AS partner to become aware of their internal levels of stress and how this is interpreted by their body and mind.

The example below shows a typical completed scale. All individuals will have a different perspective on how they rate this scale. What is important is that there is an awareness of the highest number that can be reached BEFORE control is lost. I find this is often given as six or seven. Once over this level the ability to stop the oncoming meltdown can be severely reduced. An eight or nine is maybe too late and a ten starts the meltdown.

WORKSHEET

The Stress Self-Assessment Scale (SSAS) Example

	Social event – friends crunching nibbles	
No.	**Mind**	**Body**
1	Aware of stimulus/noise	Calm but starting to become distracted
2	More aware of noise	Calm still, but noise becoming louder
3	Beginning to focus on noise	Starting to become irritated
4	Noise becoming difficult to ignore	Becoming tense
5	Focus is now upsetting	Edgy and tense
6	Trying to block it out	Blocking hearing, using distracting tactics
7	Starting to get annoyed	Blocking hearing more, feeling tense, making a counter noise
8	Need to remove myself or I don't know what I will do	Rocking, humming, total tension, irritation
9	Need to be alone or somewhere else or I will explode	Out of reasonable control. Don't know what to do
10	Do something really stupid to end it!	Fight or flight!

▄ Instructions for using the SSAS

This scale is to be completed by the AS partner.

1. Think about something that you know can cause a meltdown.

2. Start with number one, which is when you first become aware of a stressful or irritating situation.

3. Write down how your body and mind are responding at this point.

4. Work your way down the list with each number becoming more extreme.

5. Finish with ten, which would be the point you reach meltdown.

The Stress Self-Assessment Scale (SSAS)

No.	Mind	Body

When completed, share this with your partner and counsellor (if applicable). Use this chart to let your partner know what number you are so that they will know what is best to do.

Exercise for both partners to do together

Discuss together what number would allow an intervention to take place and prevent a meltdown occurring. For some, this number might be five, six or even seven. Take note of this number and decide together what could be put in place to allow the AS partner to act and prevent a meltdown reaching the point that control is lost. If it is a social event, this prevention could take the form of excusing oneself due to an early start the next day or to feeling unwell, thus allowing the AS partner to leave. If a high number is reached at home then the AS partner could retreat to another room and be allowed space and time for their brain to process and regain control. Decide together what strategy would be best and what number the AS partner would need to be before communication and togetherness continue again.

* * * *

Have a plan decided in advance so that both partners know exactly what to do if a meltdown is threatening to occur. Once again, it will be different for each individual and the plan that is decided will be dependent on the environment of the couple. For example, if the AS partner is a number five, reducing communication could be enough or maybe they could leave the room for a while or just sit somewhere quietly. Decide what works for you both. Any form of physical exercise can prove efficient at reducing stress levels, whether that is a brisk walk around the block or an intense workout in the gym. Different situations may require a different reaction; for example, plan in advance if you are going out for a meal what action a number five would require. If you both decided beforehand and the situation allows it, then putting into place these strategies can save a lot of stress and anguish. Be patient, it is worth it. Meltdowns are exhausting for both partners, and if they can be managed then both will feel more confident and safer in the relationship together.

Below is a case study giving an example of recognizing and preventing meltdown.

● CASE STUDY: BILL AND SONIA

Bill 9 (aged 38) and Sonia (aged 39). Sonia was diagnosed after autism was recognized in their daughter three years earlier. Their daughter was now ten years old. Sonia had worked hard to recognize when she was becoming overloaded and, in many ways, had learned to control this. However, she found that this control was related to how many people were in the equation, and attending social events for Bill's work colleagues or family could be a very testing time.

One evening Sonia and Bill went out to celebrate a colleague of Bill's 40th birthday at a restaurant that was not familiar to either of them. Sonia could find it difficult to manage if she found herself in unfamiliar surroundings and would agonize beforehand about how it would be. Often, she would make the effort to visit places in advance to check out the layout and be aware of any possible problems she might encounter.

Bill and Sonia had arranged for a babysitter to come over but unfortunately she was held up in traffic and did not arrive on time. Just before they were about to leave, their daughter could not find her favourite reading book and became stressed. Sonia eventually found it in the bathroom. By the time they left the house they were already ten minutes late, and Sonia's stress level was probably already at a five!

After struggling to park the car they arrived quite flustered at the restaurant and were shown to their friends' table. There were about 20 people at the table, and all were already seated. Only two seats remained – both together with their backs facing outwards. This was very difficult for Sonia as she liked to sit with her back against a wall. She found having space and people behind her very challenging. The next thing that Sonia was struggling with was the fact she was sitting opposite someone she did not know and, worse still, they had a very loud voice, which seemed to get louder as they drank more.

The restaurant had a hard wooden floor which exaggerated the acoustics to the level of an echo chamber. Sonia was finding it increasingly hard to think, concentrate and communicate, she could feel her heart pounding in her chest, all her senses were on full alert and she just wanted to scream and run away. Sonia knew she had to do something quickly, so she put her hand on Bill's arm and, leaning towards him, she simply whispered in his ear 'seven'. Sonia then took her phone from her handbag, excused herself and left. Bill followed.

The couple had discussed this strategy in advance for situations such as these if they became unmanageable for Sonia, and although it unfortunately meant telling an untruth, it was worth it to avoid what could be a very difficult and embarrassing situation if Sonia went into meltdown and lost control.

Bill joined Sonia, called for a taxi and Sonia went home. Bill returned to the table, explaining that the babysitter had called because their daughter was upset, and Sonia had caught a taxi home. He conveyed Sonia's apologies to his friend and said she wished him a lovely birthday. The group quickly restored their momentum and after a couple of drinks probably never even remembered Sonia had left.

By the time Bill arrived home Sonia had relaxed, listened to her favourite music and was back down to a safe number two.

As clearly illustrated in the case study with Bill and Sonia, social situations can be full of unpredictable events and a cocktail of sensory triggers. Forward planning and learning strategies can elevate and take away many of the unnecessary stressors. It will take time to manage and control meltdowns on any level, and putting into place strategies and coping skills can avoid much suffering, anguish, stress and embarrassment. The benefits and rewards are worth the effort for both partners. The AS individual will feel more in control and confident in managing stressful situations. By effectively managing and reducing meltdowns, they find that the negative consequences on both themselves and their partner, family and friends will be decreased. However, if anger is the dominant emotion in your relationship, whether it belongs to the AS, NT or both partners, then ways to break this cycle and bring positive change into the relationship will be vital if the relationship is going to survive. If change in the relationship is proving difficult, consider employing the help of a knowledgeable therapist to support both of you.

The area that can prove the most taxing and difficult to manage is when socializing and sharing celebrations as there are so many unpredictable variables involved. In the next chapter, strategies and coping skills will be discussed that may help make these special occasions more manageable.

• Chapter 6 •

SOCIAL INTERACTION

Being on the spectrum is a family affair

AS partners often tell me about feeling uncomfortable in social situations but not being able to determine why they have this feeling. Bearing in mind that autism causes difficulties with reading social signals and appreciating when to leave some things unsaid, this feeling of being uncomfortable may not be too uncommon for them. Sometimes an AS partner may be accused of being insensitive or tactless in their delivery of an opinion or an event. It is said of people with AS that they cannot lie. However, this is not a moral honesty; it is a straightforward delivery of a statement, often without any diplomacy. For instance, I always warn NT partners not to ask questions like 'What do you think of my new hairdo?' or 'Does my bottom look big in these jeans?' if they do not want the absolute brutal truth. NT partners become familiar with this over time and understand that their partner is not being cruel if something uncomplimentary is said, but simply offering their opinion from their perspective. Some even take comfort in the knowledge that their AS partner will always tell them what they mean and not offer false flattery.

However, other people the couple encounter in a social context do not have the benefit of this knowledge and will often be taken aback by the AS partner's brutal honesty. If they make the mistake of asking a question or seeking an opinion, they may get an answer they were not prepared for. NT partners sometimes notice the warning signs that their partner is about to say or do something inappropriate. I often suggest that the couple arrange a way for the NT partner to signal to their partner not to say it, to keep quiet and not to follow their natural impulses. This could be done with a little pinch, a cough or squeeze of the arm. It is very important this is prearranged otherwise the NT partner might find themselves in the embarrassing situation of being asked by their AS partner why they pinched them under the table! If a strategy is prearranged it can save many potential embarrassing moments and can even be amusing later, when the couple discuss what happened while they were out.

Putting together specific rules for socializing can make a difference. Having prearranged agreements and strategies in place can help prevent difficult or embarrassing moments in the future. Below is a list of some of the rules couples have made use of. This may help you construct your own list.

Important socializing rules:

- If I pinch you, it means stop saying what you are saying immediately.

- If I wink at you, it means you are doing really well.

- If I ask you 'Do you remember what you wanted to say to me?', it means change the subject and I will explain later.

- If you are feeling overloaded by the situation or becoming tired, say to me, 'I think I have a migraine coming on.' We can then excuse ourselves from the situation.

- If you feel the impulse to just leave or go home, you must tell me or send a text. Otherwise I will feel abandoned by you. I will not be cross but I will need to know where you are or how I can get home.

- If we are with other people, including family, and you take a dislike to their children, pet, partner, family, friends, appearance, hairstyle, clothes, car, job or hobby, please do not say so. We can discuss it alone later. They do not need to know of your dislike.

▬ Instructions for filling in your Important Socializing Rules worksheet

1. Take time together when you are not going to be disturbed.

2. Make sure the AS partner understands that in many situations you are their social guide and your only intention is to save both of you embarrassment or to avoid arguments.

3. Think about past cases when things have gone wrong or where there was an embarrassing situation.

4. Think how this could have been prevented.

5. Put together a list of strategies and rules that you can both work to.

6. When you have finished, check that the AS partner is not feeling put down or inferior in any way.

7. Remember that you both have different talents and it is unlikely that socializing will be the AS partner's forte, just as logical processes are not necessarily yours.

8. When it is completed, put copies up on the wall so the rules can be rehearsed and remembered. Revisit the list before a social event.

9. Start to put the rules into place as soon as possible. Practise in order for them to become part of your routine when you are out together in company.

WORKSHEET
Our Important Socializing Rules

....

....

....

....

....

....

....

....

....

....

....

When it comes to socializing, remember that word 'difference'. In Chapter 1, I used the analogy of Eagle and Zebra trying very hard to work with their differences. They had fallen in love with each other and wanted to live together. I talked about them needing a different type of food, one being carnivorous and the other herbivorous. The other difference I mentioned was the need for a different environment to live in. Eagle likes a solitary habitat far away from crowds, whereas Zebra, a herding animal, needs to be surrounded by others they can interact with.

A need for a different environment

A relationship between an AS and NT partner is not so different from Eagle and Zebra in respect of feeding and environment. The NT partner will tend to require that emotional food found in acknowledgement of them, hugging and touching or intangible, subtle expressions of devotion. The AS partner will need the logical food found in their work, business or special interests. For the majority of NT partners, living a solitary existence would be difficult, perhaps leaving them with feelings of social isolation. Likewise, for an AS partner to spend too much time in group situations, trying to be sociable, would also be very difficult and quickly use up their available resources, leading to possible meltdown.

I described earlier how the AS brain is trying to work out people and communication using logic, and how this leads to their brain working many times harder than a person who has a fully developed theory of mind. Their resources will be quickly depleted in social and group situations, as they try to figure what they are supposed to say and do, as well as what the other people around them are going to say and do. To expect the partner with AS to be able to keep up to speed in social situations and communication would only end in both feeling disappointed and let down. This is why such a major difference needs to be recognized, accepted and openly discussed, in order for both partners to spend time in their own essential environments, either alone or with others, and not feel guilty or abandoned because of it.

Having said this, it is not always just the NT partner who wants to go out and socialize – sometimes it is the AS partner who wants to go out and be among like-minded people who share their special interest. Here is a case study that explains this well and how important it is to avoid what I call the 'resentful guilt trap'.

● CASE STUDY: ANDY AND SUSAN

Andy was 49 and Susan was 53. Susan suspected Andy might be on the autistic spectrum but had not raised the issue with him. They had been living together for four years and came to counselling because they had reached a point where they could no longer communicate, and Susan was considering ending the relationship.

When they first met, Susan had admired Andy's talents as a musician. He is the lead guitarist and fiddle player in a band and was in demand to perform at various gigs. In the beginning, Susan used to go along to the gigs, and although it meant she spent most of her time alone on the sidelines, she enjoyed being there to support him. In fact, the majority of their time out together was spent at Andy's gigs.

After six months, they decided to live together. Susan had expected that Andy's time spent with his band would decrease as they became a couple and they would spend more time doing the things that she enjoyed together. This did not happen, and Andy argued that he had prearranged to do these gigs and would not let his band down by cancelling them, so he would see them through. He could not understand why Susan no longer wanted to come with him. He felt confused as she had accompanied him to most of his gigs all through their courtship and seemed really keen. Andy had presumed this would continue as Susan had not stated or indicated otherwise.

Susan liked the theatre, cinema, meals out and, best of all, curling up on the sofa to watch her favourite soaps or a good film. She also liked to please people and did not want to upset Andy by telling him that although she loved to listen to him play, she was getting quite bored with being left on her own. She was tired of having to wait around while the band packed up before they could go home, which on most nights was very late. She had been sure that once they lived together Andy would automatically want to spend more time at home and share his life with her as a couple.

Susan had managed to stay silent and tolerate the lonely late evenings at home for three-and-half-years, and although she made the occasional dig or sarcastic comment about being a music widow, Andy remained totally oblivious to her needs and did not pick up on any of the signals.

Everything reached a head one Saturday evening when Andy forgot that Susan had booked tickets for the theatre. His band called saying one of the members had been taken ill and he would be needed, so Andy instantly agreed to go. Susan was not happy about this and felt very angry and let down. Reluctantly, Andy called the band and told them he could not go. They went to the theatre, but the evening was already ruined. Andy hardly communicated at all and Susan remained annoyed with him.

As a consequence of this, Andy stopped doing a lot of the gigs he enjoyed because he realized that it upset Susan so much and he did not want to lose her. He loved Susan very much but could not understand why she had changed so drastically since they had moved in together; he felt deceived by her and decided she must be jealous of him going out with his friends. He missed being with his friends in the band very much, as it was the only time he really felt comfortable and confident within himself. He resented the sacrifice he felt he was making but believed it was not worth going out because of all the arguments and guilt trips that ensued afterwards.

Meanwhile, Susan could not understand why it was such a problem for Andy to spend time with her. She pondered that if he really loved her, she would be priority number one and he would rather be with her than out late with the band. After all, as she saw it, he had a daytime job, so why did he need extra work? However, she now felt guilty for the time she spent watching the TV as she realized that most of her favourite programmes were not enjoyed by Andy. Consequently, she had stopped watching most of them and tried to find things Andy might want to watch. Both felt bad and guilty, but also very resentful of the sacrifice they felt they were being forced to make for the other.

By the time they came to see me, both had lost touch with the other, and neither could see anything from their partner's perspective. Our work together was based on understanding and compromising. Andy was assessed positively for being on the spectrum, which brought about a much deeper understanding for both of them as to what was causing Andy's difficulties in seeing Susan's perspective and her need for his company as a couple. It also helped Susan to understand and realize how important Andy's time with his band was to him and how not being able to participate could affect his whole sense of identity and totally undermine his self-esteem. The couple worked hard to build back their relationship and I am pleased to say they did work it out together. They just needed to understand how different they were and work with that difference, not against it.

Difference can work, but only if a couple are aware of how it affects them and their relationship. This way the expectations of either partner will not exceed the reality. Sometimes, socializing for an AS/NT couple is not a problem because neither of them enjoys socializing or the NT partner has already recognized their separate need for social contact and is happy to fulfil this alone, without expecting their partner to participate. This decision can be quite difficult for some NT partners as they would really prefer that their partner shared this with them, very much in the same way their AS partner would like them to share or take part in their special interest. Some NT partners I have discussed this with say how guilty they feel leaving their partner alone, or how they feel obligated to leave an event early as their AS partner wants to go. My answer is always to say that their AS partner would probably be quite happy left alone at home to freely pursue what interests them and not have to feel guilty for doing this. The NT partner needs to recognize that their AS partner does not need to share the same environment – they will not benefit in any way from doing so – and to work with this difference. Equally, the AS partner must learn to find a balance between their needs and interests and quality couple time spent with their partner – balance being the key word.

However, it is often at special times like birthdays, Christmas and anniversaries when the need to share and celebrate the occasion together as a couple or family is especially important to the NT partner. The AS partner needs to be aware of this and ensure that they make a special effort at these times, so their NT partner is not left feeling unloved and neglected. To many AS partners, these special occasions are often regarded as just another day that comes with an overdose of stress. Special occasions for the AS partner may feel very stressful and loaded with expectations on them that they often fail to live up to, regardless of whether they make an effort or not. The AS partner is expected to plan, arrange, buy, wrap and pre-empt their partner's wishes without any information or clues whatsoever. Total autistic nightmare.

Celebrations

Some NT partners have reported not receiving a card, let alone a present, for their birthday or Christmas, and this seems even more likely to happen if the AS partner is male. This may be due to upbringing; perhaps cards, presents and celebrating special occasions were not part of the AS partner's childhood. Another reason may be because they are not particularly bothered about receiving anything, so find it difficult to appreciate why anyone else would want to receive these things.

One reason people give gifts and cards is because the other person's happiness makes them happy. The very act of giving, even if the gift or card is not to the receiver's taste, does please. In addition, the AS partner may struggle to figure out what their partner wants to receive and may become anxious about getting it right. This need to get it right coupled with the fear of getting it wrong can be the reason why the AS partner doesn't risk buying anything at all. The AS partner may find it very hard to imagine what it is their partner would like to receive. Trying to think of presents and surprises without any clues or instructions can be nigh on impossible for them.

When I discuss this with clients, the AS partner will often say, 'Why can't they [partner] just say what they want, and I can just go and get it?' This is a very logical solution to the problem. However, it does not suit all NT partners who then feel deprived of the emotional aspect of a surprise gift. For the NT partner, receiving gifts is an emotional experience as well as a practical one. NT partners can feel valued if their partner has put some effort and time into the gift, and the surprise is always a pleasure.

By the same token, having the NT partner turn around and say 'I'd like a bracelet for my birthday' is a potential time bomb for the AS partner. It will be a source of great stress and anxiety as the AS partner will be unable to imagine what kind of bracelet their partner would like. Torment over what the NT partner expects the bracelet to be like, or how much money it should cost, will ensue.

Special occasions can be a source of anxiety, stress and hurt feelings for both partners. There is, however, a way round this that I have developed and found to be quite successful. The NT partner needs to give their AS partner a list of, let's say, ten things they'd like to receive, any of which would be a pleasure to have. This way, the AS partner will know exactly what to get and the NT partner will still have the surprise of not knowing what will be chosen from the list. Below I have set out an example and then a blank copy of a birthday, Christmas and anniversary sheet. If you belong to a culture that has different celebrations which involve giving gifts, then there is a blank sheet for you to fill in.

WORKSHEET

Birthday Presents (Example)

PRESENT Slippers

Where to buy it .Marks...

Price .10-15...

Size/type/colour .8 – Red or Black...

PRESENT Pyjamas

Where to buy it .Marks...

Price .20-25...

Size/type/colour .16 – Red or Black...

PRESENT Treatment at Spa

Where to buy it .Longly Spa Hotel...

Price .50-75...

Size/type/colour ....

PRESENT X Box Game Heroes

Where to buy it .Archers Game Centre...

Price .49.99...

Size/type/colour ....

▬ Instructions for filling in the present list – for the NT partner

1. Complete the appropriate list at least one month before the date of the celebration.

2. Be sure that all gifts are equally desired.

3. Be very accurate with the present, where to buy it, colour, size and so on, and, above all, be clear about the price range. You could put, say, no more than £25 or between £10 and £15.

4. Do not under any circumstances say after the event that you wish something else had been chosen from the list.

▬ Instructions for buying a present from the list – for the AS partner

1. Choose one (or more) of the presents you would like to buy your partner.

2. Take time to be sure you have read the list accurately.

3. Make sure you hide the present in a safe place.

4. Do not give any clues as to what the present is.

5. Disguise the present when you wrap it, so your partner will not be able to guess what it is; for instance, put it in a bigger box.

6. Take time to choose some nice paper and a card.

7. Write a nice message on the card.

Birthday Presents

PRESENT

Where to buy it ....

Price ....

Size/type/colour ....

PRESENT

Where to buy it ....

Price ....

Size/type/colour ....

PRESENT

Where to buy it ....

Price ....

Size/type/colour ....

PRESENT

Where to buy it ....

Price ....

Size/type/colour ....

WORKSHEET
Christmas Presents

PRESENT

Where to buy it . . . .

Price . . . .

Size/type/colour . . . .

PRESENT

Where to buy it . . . .

Price . . . .

Size/type/colour . . . .

PRESENT

Where to buy it . . . .

Price . . . .

Size/type/colour . . . .

PRESENT

Where to buy it . . . .

Price . . . .

Size/type/colour . . . .

WORKSHEET

Anniversary Presents

PRESENT

Where to buy it . . . .

Price . . . .

Size/type/colour . . . .

PRESENT

Where to buy it . . . .

Price . . . .

Size/type/colour . . . .

PRESENT

Where to buy it . . . .

Price . . . .

Size/type/colour . . . .

PRESENT

Where to buy it . . . .

Price . . . .

Size/type/colour . . . .

WORKSHEET

Presents for Other Occasions

PRESENT

Where to buy it ....

Price ....

Size/type/colour ....

PRESENT

Where to buy it ....

Price ....

Size/type/colour ....

PRESENT

Where to buy it ....

Price ....

Size/type/colour ....

PRESENT

Where to buy it ....

Price ....

Size/type/colour ....

Completing these lists for the AS partner can offer much relief and feel as though a tremendous pressure has lifted for them. All the guesswork and risk of failure are removed. The NT partner still has the element of surprise as they won't know which gift their partner has chosen. The majority of AS partners I see say they just want to make their partner happy. Unfortunately, many struggle to figure out how, but at least knowing what their partner would like as a gift can make such a difference to them both. Using specific lists like these can make happy occasions happier.

It is very important that the NT partner does not feel impolite or selfish about the items listed. It might take time to get used to doing this, as it is often easier to give than receive. It really does make things so much easier for the AS partner. Both will gain from the removal of the pressure and guesswork in choosing and the fear of disappointing. These lists can also be given to the AS partner to fill in, as in some cases the NT partner also finds it a struggle to predict what would be an appropriate gift to make their AS partner happy.

Arranging surprise celebrations

The other area where lists can prove useful is in arranging surprise evenings or days out. Many NT clients have stated that they feel responsible for making all the social arrangements; that if they did not arrange things they would never go anywhere. This can leave the NT partner feeling, once again, unloved and undervalued. They often yearn for their partners to do something for them and to show they are important enough to spoil them every now and then. It's not a lot to ask, you may think. However, once again, the decision of what to choose – fearing they might disappoint – makes it very difficult for the AS partner. Basically, the AS partner needs to know what their NT partner would like to do. Without information and instructions it is unlikely that the AS partner will succeed at this task and the surprise night out that the NT partner desperately wants may not happen. The AS partner may have memories of failed evenings in the past and does not want to risk further confrontation or feelings of failure.

Once again, a simple list can help change all this and make a positive difference to both. Below are instructions, followed by an example of a 'places to celebrate' list which the NT partner can fill in. It may also be useful for the AS partner to fill in these lists, in order to maintain a balance in the relationship.

▬ Instructions for filling in the surprise celebrations list – for the NT (or AS) partner

1. Have at least four places on the list at all times.

2. Be sure that any of the places or events is somewhere you would equally like to go.

3. Be accurate about the venue and any special things you like at certain places.

4. Under no circumstances say after the event that you wish something else had been chosen.

WORKSHEET
Surprise Celebrations

Place or event ....

Location ....

Things I like ....

Date or days ....

Place or event ....

Location ....

Things I like ....

Date or days ....

Place or event ....

Location ....

Things I like ....

Date or days ....

Place or event ....

Location ....

Things I like ....

Date or days ....

So much is about finding out what works for you and your family. It is about experimenting, and sometimes using trial and error. Making rules and establishing strategies can work wonders in an AS/NT relationship. However, sometimes a new situation comes up where the old strategy needs to be adjusted to fit it. This is called putting things into context.

Getting the context right

Rules and strategies are useful as they work well within an AS/NT relationship. However, no rule can deal with all situations and, at times, adjustments need to be made. The AS partner may find this difficult as they can tend to be reluctant to make changes. For example, the AS partner might not know when their NT partner wants a hug. The couple may have a rule that if one of them is crying then that means they want a hug. This is fine until it is something the AS partner has done which has left the NT partner angry and in tears. The AS partner coming over to hug may elicit a sharp response. An adjustment to the rule might be that when the NT partner is crying the AS partner actually says 'Hug?' before trying to.

Some NT partners complain that their AS partner learns very little from social situations, that they are weary of continually reinforcing the learning and adapting to new situations. Unfortunately, there is little that can be done about this. The NT partner will in many ways be the social guide in the relationship. I try to put this in perspective by asking, 'If your partner was visually impaired, would you expect them to automatically know where things were in an unfamiliar environment?' Looking at it this way helps improve the understanding of why things happen as they do. This is not due to the AS partner's reluctance to try; it is due to being on the autistic spectrum, which makes certain things difficult to achieve. This does not excuse the AS partner from trying to learn or adapt to situations they find themselves in – quite the contrary. If the NT partner sees efforts being made, even if those efforts are not quite right, the feeling of being alone is eased.

Maintenance of the relationship, as I discuss in Chapter 16, should not be left entirely up to the NT partner, and I have worked with many AS partners who try very hard to adapt, understand and in general fit in with family and social life. However, this is not easy for the AS partner, as in social circumstances, they will not just be dealing with the unpredictability and sometimes very unfamiliar environments, they will also be trying to manage the surge of sensory stimuli that is pouring over them. Sensory sensitivity is very real and can often totally overwhelm AS individuals, causing meltdown and confusion for everyone.

• Chapter 7 •

SENSORY SENSITIVITY

S ENSORY sensitivity affects many individuals who are on the spectrum. However, it can also affect individuals who do not have an autistic spectrum condition. It needs to be remembered that autism is a spectrum condition that consists of multiple traits; in other words, you have to get a lot of ticks in a lot of boxes to be diagnosed with autism. Therefore, although being affected by sensory sensitivity is a strong indication of autism, an individual would need to have a number of other autistic traits alongside sensory sensitivity in order to meet the criteria of having an autistic spectrum condition.

Until May 2013, sensory sensitivity did not appear in the *Diagnostic and Statistical Manual (DSM)*, and the *DSM-IV* criteria for an autistic condition made no mention of sensory sensitivity. The *DSM* is a manual, published by the American Psychiatric Association, which lists all the relevant symptoms for a diagnosis of each disorder. It is only since the publication of the *DSM-5* in 2013 that sensory sensitivity has found a well-deserved place in the diagnostic criteria.

Reactions to sensory sensitivity can be hyperactive or hypoactive; for example, the AS individual may react strongly to noises that are inaudible to others or it could be that the AS individual shows little reaction or awareness to pain that would be intolerable to a non-AS individual. I have worked with clients who could not be in a room with a clock ticking, even if others could not hear it. Equally, I have known clients who were able to have teeth drilled or extracted and report little or no pain! This aspect of autism certainly does not make life easy for AS individuals, who not only are having to cope with the ambiguities of people and communication, but are also bombarded with overwhelming stimuli at every turn and often with no escape!

For example, travelling on the Underground for some is an everyday activity, but for someone on the spectrum it can be a sensory nightmare. Consider for a moment the abundance of sensory stimuli that using the Underground system will create: the smells of people clustered together, the heat of a packed carriage, people eating food, crunching, munching, people pushing past, being forced into physical contact with people, noise echoing around you not just from the train but also from people trying to shout over each other but speakers blasting out instructions and announcements. Add to this fluorescent lights burning above, spreading a cascade of auras and flickering brightness, and the almost tangible taste of the atmosphere and body odours. It sounds like a nightmare! For the AS individual, it often is. For those with sensory sensitivity, everyday events can result in an overwhelming assault on the senses that can be very difficult to manage.

Sensory sensitivity is a reality for the majority of individuals on the autistic spectrum and can have a profound effect on stress and anxiety levels, which in turn can affect the capacity to cope and may trigger a meltdown.

The problems, pain and anguish caused by the senses are not always disclosed or spoken about by the AS individual, which can leave their partner confused as to what is the matter and what it is that is causing their partner to feel stressed. Many AS individuals have learned that not everyone is as negatively affected by the sensory stressors as they are. Unfortunately, the learning has also been that others are not very understanding or sympathetic towards their struggles. They might have experience, as a man, of being told not to act like such a wimp or to man up, or as a woman, being viewed as complaining or neurotic. Hence many have learned to put on the mask and hide how they feel, or try to avoid the irritant that causes them problems. Here is a short case study that helps put this into context.

● CASE STUDY: ROB AND MADELINE

Rob, aged 63, and Madeline, aged 59, first met six years ago on a dating site. They were attracted to each other from the outset and their relationship quickly became serious. Madeline was attracted to Rob's 'difference' as she called it; he was quite unlike any man she had ever known, as he was comfortable with his feminine side and treated everyone as an equal. He had a very strong sense of loyalty to the people that mattered to him and this was something they shared together. They also shared a love of reading and film, although trying to get Rob to go along to their local cinema had proved hopeless.

Rob would insist on waiting until a film came out on DVD, which did not make Madeline happy as she loved the whole experience of going to the cinema including the popcorn and cinema treats! Madeline started to make a point about Rob's refusal. She argued that she always went with him to visit the battlegrounds of the Great Wars, so why could he not join her to see a film at the cinema? Eventually, Rob gave in and agreed to go as Madeline had arranged to take the grandchildren to the cinema and didn't want to take them alone.

It was a Disney film and Madeline had arranged to take their three grandchildren, who were very excited that 'Grandpa' Rob was coming along for the first time. They arrived at the cinema in good time as Madeline was aware that time was very important to Rob. Madeline was also aware that Rob had not slept well the night before and had been tense all day. He seemed agitated and was quite short with her when she pointed out he was driving a little too fast to the cinema.

Once the tickets had been purchased, Madeline and the grandchildren joined the queue for popcorn and treats, the children excitedly choosing their tubs of popcorn, snacks and sweets. Madeline treated herself to a bag of cheesy tortilla chips. Into the cinema they went, found their allocated seats in the centre row and eagerly waited for the film to start. Within no time at all, the whole cinema was alive with crunching popcorn, rustling bags, slurping drinks. Rob began to shuffle around in his seat and Madeline was aware that he kept cupping his hands over his ears. She offered him a tortilla chip and was surprised when he suddenly stood up and, saying sorry, hastily made his way to the exit.

Madeline thought he had gone to the toilet, but when he didn't return, she became concerned. She did not want to leave the children alone in the cinema and really did not know what to do. She had depended on Rob being there so that they could take it in turns to take the children to the toilet. When the youngest wanted to use the toilet, Madeline had to take all three with her.

She found Rob sat outside in the foyer looking very forlorn and lost, his head in his hands. She asked if he was feeling unwell and Rob replied that he would talk to her later.

When the children had been dropped off with their respective parents, Rob and Madeline returned home. For the first time, Rob explained to Madeline how excruciating the noise was for him, in particular the rustling bags and the crunching. At first, Madeline thought he was making a joke and she wasn't sure how to respond, but when Rob went on to explain how loud and painful the noise felt to his ears, making it impossible to concentrate on the film, she took him seriously. Although he had not been diagnosed, both had long been aware that Rob was on the spectrum, but this was something he had never mentioned before, because he said he didn't want Madeline to think he was being some sort of a freak. Madeline had once worked with children on the spectrum as a teacher, so was all too aware of sensory issues, but she had never put Rob in that category. Now that she knew, she could make better sense of why he avoided certain things and why he always made an excuse to leave the room when she ate a bag of crisps at home.

Initially, Rob had been reluctant to disclose in detail how specific noises made him feel and the sometimes profound effect they had on his mood, stress, anger level and general ability to cope. It was very important that he felt safe enough to be totally honest and open with Madeline and share with confidence and without any fear of being ridiculed his reaction to specific noises. Once Madeline understood, they worked together to put strategies in place to prevent Rob being put in a situation that became overwhelming and unbearable for him.

This case study highlights just one way a person on the spectrum may be affected by sensory sensitivity. There are, of course, many other ways that this trait of autism might present itself.

Being aware of sensory issues

It is important to be aware of the sensory issues that affect the AS partner, and I have compiled a questionnaire below for each of the senses for the AS partner to complete and then share with their partner.

▬ Instructions for completing the Sensory Sensitivity Questionnaire

Exercise to be completed by the AS partner.

1. Find a time you can sit quietly and not be disturbed.

2. Look through the following questionnaire for the different senses.

3. Tick the type of stimulus that you are affected by in an adverse or irritating way.

4. If it is not mentioned, then enter it in the appropriate blank space.

5. In the next column, allocate a number between 1 and 10 to indicate how stressful and irritating this noise is to you, 1 being the lowest stress level and 10 being the highest. For example, if you are adversely affected by people chewing food, then you would tick that box and give it a 9 or 10. If, however, chewing only bothered you slightly, you would give it a 2 or 3.

6. If there are any sensory issues not included, add them to the blank rows provided.

7. When you have finished your questionnaire, share it with your partner and discuss how you both might work out a way to alleviate the sensory effect.

The Sensory Sensitivity Questionnaire (SSQ)

NOISE

Please tick the appropriate box corresponding to the type of noise that has a negative impact on you. Add a number for how stressful it feels: 1 being the lowest stress and 10 being the highest stress level. If something is not mentioned that affects you, then enter it in the blank spaces provided.	Yes	Stress level
Sniffing		
Breathing		
Sneezing		
Babies crying		
Children screaming, shrieking, laughing		
Chewing		
Crunching (apples, raw vegetables, crispbread)		
Munching (popcorn, crisps, biscuits)		
Slurping (drinks)		
Cat meowing		
Dog barking		
Bird noises		
Cat/dog licking/cleaning itself		
Clanging cutlery		
Ticking clocks		
Dripping water		
Rustling (crisp bags, packets)		
Car windscreen wipers		
Fans		
Air conditioning		
Heaters		
Fridges		
Hairdryers		
Hand dryers		
Vacuum cleaners		
House/car/smoke alarms		

Drills and tools		
Sirens, Underground trains		
Car/lorry horns		
Whistles		
Fireworks		
Typing – keyboard		
People talking in the background		
Furniture scraping		
Echoing environments		
General background noise:		

TOUCH

Please tick the appropriate box corresponding to the type of touch that has an impact on you. Add a number for how stressful it feels: 1 being the lowest stress and 10 being the highest stress level. If something is not mentioned that affects you, then enter it in the blank spaces below.	Yes	Stress level
Wool		
Nylon		
Cotton wool		
Feathers		
Playdoh		
Latex		
Polystyrene		
Rubber		
Tickling		

	Yes	Stress level
Hugging		
Hair being brushed		
Labels in clothes		
Animal fur		
The feel and texture of certain foods in the mouth:		
Mushrooms		
Creamy foods		
Seedy fruit, strawberries, raspberries		
Pickled beetroot		
Overcooked meat		
Slippery fruit, lychees, plums		

TASTE AND SMELL

	Yes	Stress level
Please tick the appropriate box corresponding to the type of tastes and smells listed. Add a number for how stressful it feels: 1 being the lowest stress and 10 being the highest stress level. If something is not mentioned that affects you, then enter it in the blank spaces below.		
Taste of certain foods:		
Taste of lipstick/lip balm		
Food smells:		
Cooking smells:		
Smell of urine		
Bleach		
The smell of people's breath		

	Yes	Stress level
Specific perfumes		
Nail polish		
Nail polish remover		
Hairspray		

SIGHT – VISUAL

Please tick the appropriate box corresponding to the type of visual stress listed below. Add a number for how stressful it feels: 1 being the lowest stress and 10 being the highest stress level. If something is not mentioned that affects you, then enter it in the blank spaces below.	Yes	Stress level
Fluorescent lights		
Sunlight		
Headlights		
Lasers		
Flashing lights		
The sight of someone eating		
Being pointed at		
Eye contact		
Cinema and theatre: exit signs, step lights		
Specific colours		

Once you have completed the questionnaire, share it with your partner and discuss ways that you might reduce the adverse effects of the overwhelming stimuli.

We will now consider some suggestions to alleviate the impact of negative stimuli.

Ways to reduce the impact of negative stimuli
Noise

- Wear ear plugs at night to block out the sound of breathing.

- Put crisps and popcorn in a container to avoid the rustling sound of the bags.

- Use headphones or the playing of music to block out background noise in noisy places or situations where difficult sounds are expected, such as walking alongside a busy road.

- Move away from the source/location of difficult sounds when possible.

- Have a prepared excuse to tell people if you need to leave an environment where noise is a problem.

- Agree with work that lunch can be eaten away from others, for example at a desk, if the noise of people eating is a problem.

- Arrange to meet people in places you know are quiet.

- Have a quiet place to work or study where possible.

- Choose an aisle seat in the cinema or theatre.

Touch

- Communicate to those around you which touches are acceptable/not acceptable.

- Ask those around you to check out if a touch is acceptable first before touching you.

- Cut out labels in clothes.

- Choose clothes made of fabrics that are tolerable.

Taste

- Carry around chewing gum, a mouth freshener or toothpaste to use if you have eaten something you don't like the taste of.

Smell

- Try to avoid standing directly in front of someone if the smell of their breath is a problem.

- Buy gentle cleaning products that do not smell too harshly.

- Carry around a scent you find relaxing, such as moisturiser, oil or spray and use it to help mask and block out other unpleasant smells.

Visual

- When eating, try to sit beside your partner/friends rather than opposite them.

- Wear sunglasses if bright light is a problem.

- Get a dimmer switch for lights in the house.

- Fit blackout curtains in the bedroom.

Of the five sensitivities, noise appears to be the most common in both men and women on the spectrum. Sensitivity to noise, particularly oral noise, such as chewing, breathing and sniffling, is also known as misophonia and is a condition that can exist on its own, in the absence of autism. Misophonia can have a profound impact on a person's social life and make eating out and celebrations a nightmare. In severe cases, it can have a strong adverse effect on the couple's relationship. If the AS partner cannot cope with being in the same room as their partner or family while they eat or cannot share a bed because of the sound of their partner breathing, then the impact on the relationship can be distancing, confusing and detrimental. Understanding the cause can help families to manage better.

The adverse effect of noises can take many forms, as is illustrated in the questionnaire. These noises are often repetitive, such as the ticking of a clock, the dripping of a tap or the swishing noise made by windscreen wipers. They can become a major distraction to AS individuals, making it almost impossible for them to concentrate on the task in hand, and can lead to them being held responsible for conversations being misheard and missed. This is just one of the reasons why the NT partner needs to be aware of their partner's sensitivity to specific distractions in the environment so that they can choose the right environment in which to have important discussions or give relevant messages or instructions. It is also important that the AS partner is able to say when they are distracted and not able to concentrate, rather than just nodding in agreement and hoping for the best!

There are numerous reasons why the AS partner may not speak up and disclose when they have not heard or understood an instruction. The most common reason is the AS partner's fear of confrontation! They fear that if they keep saying 'pardon' or ask their partner to repeat what they have just said, their partner will be annoyed, dismissive or make them feel stupid or incompetent. The reality is that if their partner understands why this happens, they will be much less likely to mind being asked to give more details and repeat themselves. This avoids the disappointment and inconvenience of the instructions not being carried out or being misunderstood.

Using the written word rather than the spoken word can be a tremendous benefit to couples affected by a spectrum condition. Using the questionnaire in this chapter and rating the effect of sensory sensitivity in numbers can help the NT partner to become more aware of their partner's world and the daily irritations that they encounter.

A note for therapists

Issues caused by sensory sensitivity also carry strong implications for therapy. For any couple or individual on the autistic spectrum who is looking to attend therapy, it is essential that attention is given to the environment that therapy will be delivered in. Consider the following practicalities:

- How are the chairs positioned? Facing the therapist directly can feel uncomfortable or intimidating for some AS individuals.

- How does the room smell? I have learned over the years not to use air fresheners in the therapy room.

- How is the room lit? Is the lighting too harsh or too bright?

- Are there windows in the room? Activity outside can be distracting.

- Are there fans or heaters being used in the room? Certain noises can be irritating as well as distracting.

- Are there noises in the room, such as the ticking of clocks?

- Are there noises outside the room? External noises can feel disturbing and prevent concentration.

If therapy is going to be productive and beneficial for individuals on the spectrum, then all these practicalities need to be taken seriously and considered. If possible, the environment will need to be adapted to offer the AS client the best possible chance of feeling relaxed, stress free and safe.

The therapist will need to address any issues in the first session otherwise they might find that their client does not return. This consideration for the comfort of the AS client is also relevant to medical consultations, job interviews and job reviews.

One area where an awareness of sensory sensitivity is crucial is in the intimate and sexual aspects of the relationship, as it is this area where most of the senses will come into play and be affected.

• Chapter 8 •

SEXUAL ISSUES

THIS is an area that seems either to work very well or is fraught with difficulties for AS/NT relationships. If you fall into the former category, then this chapter may not be applicable to you. The most common comments made by NT partners are of feeling either sexually used or sexually deprived. They talk about feelings of not being desired, being undervalued and that their partner is no longer attracted to them. There is a greater prevalence of this when the AS partner is male and the NT partner is female.

Making each other feel good, offering affection and acknowledging the positives each brings are all part of building intimacy. When I ask the AS adult what he values about his partner, he will often proceed to tell me what his partner does, such as being a good wife, cook or mother, rather than telling me who their partner is and their positive characteristics. In my book *What Men with Asperger Syndrome Want to Know About Women, Dating and Relationships* (2012), I discuss (Chapters 29 to 31) the importance of the AS partner making their NT partner feel special and loved. I cover this under three titles: 'Why are cards and gifts so important to her?', 'Why does she need me to keep telling her I love her?' and 'How can I keep saying "I love you" and other nice things without sounding false?' This book was specifically written for men on the spectrum and covers these and many other questions a man on the spectrum might ask about women.

It often came as a great surprise for many of my AS clients to realize the importance of making their partner feel special and just how closely linked giving positive reinforcement was to whether lovemaking would be likely to result. Showing a partner that their qualities and attributes are acknowledged and valued confirms that they are appreciated for the person they are, rather than for the things they do like cooking or cleaning. For example, rather than telling his partner she does a good job looking after the children, he could say to her, 'You are such a caring, patient and understanding person and that shows so much in how you are with the children. You are a wonderful mother to our children.' Showing a partner that you acknowledge their qualities and admire and respect them for how they demonstrate and share those positives with others confirms to them that you appreciate who they are, which is the reason they do the things they do. It is these affirmations that help to build closeness and intimacy between a couple. It is being made to feel special and appreciated for who they are.

It is not only verbal affirmations that bring a couple close together, but also physical affirmations, or affection. Affection can play a critical role in whether making love takes place, and being on the spectrum does not determine whether someone is demonstrative and tactile in their approach to lovemaking – any more than it makes someone a good lover or a poor lover. Many of these factors are down to the individual and their needs, desires and personality. All the couples I have worked with have been different in their perceptions, attitude and how much they prioritize lovemaking and affection.

Just as I have listened to accounts from the NT partner as to how deprived of affection and intimacy they feel, I have also listened to accounts of their AS partners being too affectionate and needing constant physical affirmation from them that they are loved. Others report that the sexual side of their relationship is just right and the most uncomplicated aspect of their relationship. All individuals are different, regardless of whether they are affected by an ASC. All individuals have different sexual appetites and varying libidos and differ in how much relevance they place on sex. If a couple's needs and desires are matched then the sexual side of the relationship will work, even if that means there is little or no sex between the couple. If, however, a couple have very different views and needs regarding sex, it can cause disharmony in their relationship.

It can be either partner who puts less emphasis on the sex relationship and withdraws. This may be due to a low libido or, for the NT partner, it is frequently because they do not feel emotionally supported and made to feel special enough, which will be discussed later in this chapter.

Being on the spectrum cannot be held directly responsible for a neglectful sex life but it can indirectly play a part in making it difficult for the AS partner to initiate or maintain it. This may be due to complications in communication, reading non-verbal signals, being overly concerned with getting it right, being distracted and sensory sensitivity. All of these can play havoc with the smooth running of the couple's sexual relationship, causing it, in some cases, to cease altogether.

First, let us look at body language and the difficulty AS individuals can have on reading the signs. Sex is a form of communication and, as we already know, this can be difficult for the AS partner. Getting the timing right, trying to read their partner's sexual signals or figuring out what is wanted of them are all a bit of a nightmare. Sometimes the AS partner may decide that because they feel like making love then their partner must do too. Again, this is due to lack of theory of mind, the inability to appreciate that someone else can have a different mindset to one's own.

Using colours or a 'traffic light system' can work quite well: for instance, green can mean 'yes, I want you'; amber, 'I am thinking about it, let's see what happens'; and red means 'no, I would just like a cuddle tonight'. A colour for desire can also be agreed between the couple. For instance, say the colour is purple – it can then be added to the feelings in colour system I discussed in Chapter 3. Each could then indicate their sexual desire through saying something like: 'My colour purple is eight tonight. What's yours?' A word of warning here. It is important with either the traffic lights or the level of the desire colour that neither partner feels pressurized or rejected by their partner's response. At all times, whatever the outcome, the couple should try and cuddle.

Another way is to use an obvious, mutually agreed sign, such as for the NT partner to say, 'If I take my nightdress off or place your hand on my breast, I really desire you and making love would be nice.' Again, it must be agreed that this does not mean the AS partner has to have sex, and must feel free to say no; sometimes a cuddle is just as satisfying.

Another problem NT partners express is a feeling that they have a low libido because they are not wooed by their partner or made to feel physically special. I have heard NT women say, 'Why would I want to make love to someone who's barely said two words to me all day?' Of course, we're back to the same problem of our AS partner not knowing what they are supposed to say or do, or when to do it! There is also a tendency to worry about getting things wrong, and this could prevent the AS partner from even trying to initiate sex. Consequently, the NT partner may feel that all the responsibility for initiating lovemaking lies with them. However, on the obverse, the NT partner may find it difficult or uncomfortable to have to ask or tell their partner when they want to make love. For many, the very act of asking works as an indirect passion killer, resulting in even more feelings of not being special.

Making a partner feel special

I have compiled a short list of suggestions below that the AS partner could use to make the NT partner feel special. Obviously, making your own list will make the suggestions more personal and individual. Use the list to make one another feel special. You could even designate specific days to each other. In this way, our AS partner will know when it is their turn to do something special.

Some suggestions for making a partner feel special

- Say something nice about your partner's physical appearance or attire.

- Offer your partner a hug.

- Hold your partner's hand when out walking together or sitting together.

- Bring home flowers, a rose, a plant, a gift.

- Include a little card on which you have written a nice message.

- Give or post your partner a card to say how much you appreciate them.

- Run a nice hot bath and put some oils or fragrant bubble bath in it.

- Light some candles in the bathroom to make it even more romantic.

- Light candles and turn the lights down to create a romantic atmosphere and set the scene for intimacy.

- Give your partner a massage. Spend time over this and use fragrant oils.

- Tell your partner you love them, even if you have already told them this before or earlier in the day.

- Try and tell them the things you love them for.

Taking time for each other, offering affection and finding ways to make your partner feel special will give your relationship the vital vitamins and minerals it needs to maintain itself and stay healthy. Couples need to feed their relationship just as they need to feed their bodies, otherwise ill-health and starvation will be the results.

From the many accounts I have received, there appears to be a pattern emerging as the transition from the 'courtship stage' to the 'living together stage' progresses in relationships. In the early stages of the relationship, the NT partner describes the tremendous effort that was made to make them feel special, and most feel they were top of their new partner's priority list. I hear descriptions of gifts, cards, flowers, outings, holidays and some very thoughtful gestures being made by the AS partner. Unfortunately, once the relationship is established and the couple live together, the attention and displays of affection can end quite abruptly as the AS partner rapidly becomes refocused on their special interest or work. The courtship stage is suddenly over and the NT partner finds themselves feeling neglected and bottom of their partner's priority list, left yearning for what they once had. This is especially the case if the NT partner is female, regardless of whether they are in a heterosexual or lesbian relationship.

■ Instructions for filling in the Wooing List

1. Make some time together to fill out a list.

2. Both think of ideas you would like to do or have your partner do that would make you feel loved, desired and valued.

3. You can have a list each or combine your lists together.

WORKSHEET
Our Wooing List

....

....

....

....

....

....

....

....

....

....

....

....

....

....

....

You will need to experiment until you find what works for you. Sometimes the sexual side of a relationship can be a real problem due to the AS partner being affected by sensory sensitivity. This may be more likely when the AS partner is female.

Sensory sensitivity

I have already discussed sensory sensitivity in the previous chapter; however, I do feel that it is worth revisiting when exploring sexual issues as it is responsible for many of the problems that can arise in the bedroom. Sensory sensitivity can present itself in various forms. It can affect any of the senses – sight, hearing, smell, taste and touch. Sometimes the AS partner may not realize they are affected, presuming that everyone else is the same. This can result in them not talking about how something makes them feel, presuming their partner already knows.

One male NT partner told me how his female AS partner would push him away whenever he tried to touch her breasts. He assured me that his partner's breasts were beautiful, and he had told her so. He also added that he was very gentle. What he did not realize was that to his partner this gentle touching was irritating and unpleasant. Sensory sensitivity can cause an extreme, almost painful reaction to being touched in a specific way in specific places. This can be any part of the body. However, the most common areas for women are the nipples, clitoris, arms and ears. For some AS men, it can be the penis, and it may be painful for them when they climax, or irritating if touched in a certain way.

As well as *where* the AS partner is touched, *how* they are touched can equally make the difference to the experience being painful, irritating or – the desired response – pleasurable. Sometimes the problem is the way in which one partner actually touches the other. Often it is the gentle, tickling, stroking movements that can cause the most extreme reaction, and the longer this goes on, the worse it can feel. Ask the AS partner to demonstrate how they would touch themselves. Learn from this, practise and be guided by them. It is their body, after all, and they will be the expert on how they like to be touched. Finding a way to touch that does not cause such a negative reaction or restricting touch to safe parts of the body can eliminate this problem.

When I work with couples regarding the sexual side of the relationship, I often find that touch is the main issue that arises for both partners. For the AS partner, it is finding touch in specific areas as very unpleasant or at times unbearable. Often these areas of heightened sensitivity are the erogenous zones, and if their NT partner is not aware, of this, they are likely to home in on these areas when trying to pleasure their partner. This can and has caused many problems for both if the NT partner is not aware as they could feel quite hurt if their advances are rebuffed or rejected. The second piece of information that would be useful for the NT partner to be aware of is how their partner wants to be touched. For some AS individuals, a slight touch or a tickle can be excruciating and be very stress inducing for them if applied to specific parts of their body. Equally, being too rough or using too much pressure can have a similar effect.

NT partners may feel this is depriving them of the pleasure they receive from touching and caressing their partner's erogenous zones, not understanding how uncomfortable it can be for the AS partner. In response to this, I may ask them to imagine how it would feel to have their penis or nipples rubbed with wire wool. This normally gets the message across. Sensory sensitivity is very real for the AS partner. It is important to respect this and not force change that could upset or alienate.

Trying to communicate where to touch and how to touch can be very difficult and stressful for the AS partner, so stressful that often they don't communicate the information at all, but just say nothing and avoid physical and intimate contact all together. If this happens, the NT partner will be even more confused and may feel very hurt and rebuffed by their partner, leading them to feel unwanted and unloved.

For AS/NT couples, I have created a method called 'body maps' that does not require verbal communication. Body maps are a visual way to allow couples to show rather than tell their partners what they prefer and how. They are a blank diagram of the body from the back and front, and there is one for each partner to fill in. Each partner colours in the parts of their body where they like to be touched and the parts they do not. When I do this exercise, I also include the NT partner and ask them to fill one out too. Making love is a two-way act and the AS partner is frequently very pleased to have a foolproof map of their partner's body to refer to. Once the body map is completed by both partners, they share their body maps and, if they wish, can discuss them together. This is then followed by another copy of a blank body map which is coloured in according to how touch is preferred in certain zones of the body. Once again, when completed by both, the body maps are exchanged and discussed if desired. On the following page are two examples of a completed body map. Body Map 1 is about *where* you like to be touched, and Body Map 2 is about *how* you like to be touched.

This Body Map 1 example shows *where* touch is pleasant and *where* it should be avoided.

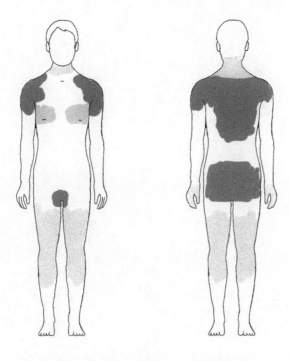

Red = pleasant touch
Blue = to be avoided

This Body Map 2 example shows *how* touch is preferred, and whether hard pressure or light pressure is preferred.

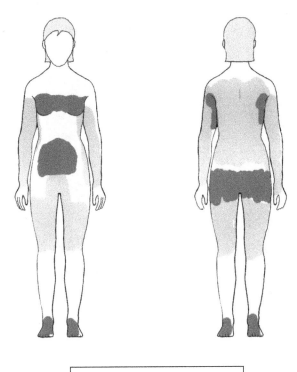

Red = firm/hard pressure
Blue = light pressure

▬ Instructions for using the body maps for the AS and NT partner

1. Complete these maps when you will not be disturbed, and phones are turned off.

2. Do not complete these body maps when you are both expecting to make love straight away as they might take time to process.

3. Complete Body Map 1. Use a different colour for the areas where you like to be touched and areas that should be avoided.

4. Complete Body Map 2. Use a different colour for how you like to be touched either with a light pressure or a firm pressure.

5. Share your body maps with each other.

Body Map 1: Fill in using one colour for areas where you like to be touched and another colour for areas that should be avoided.

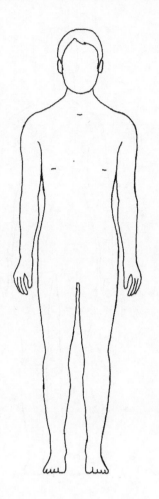
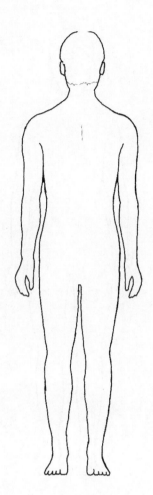

Body Map 2: Fill in using one colour for areas you like to be touched with a firm pressure and another colour for areas you like to be touched with a light pressure.

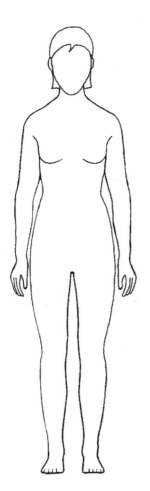
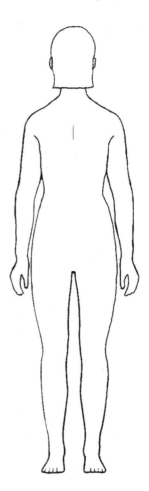

Spend time exploring your maps together; they are a map of your partner's body that will allow each of you to know with confidence that you are giving your partner the pleasure they desire. These maps can remove months and sometimes years of not knowing whether you are both getting it right. By making the exercise visual, the body maps take away the whole awkwardness of finding the right words to explain a sensitive topic and hence reduce the fear, for both, of getting it wrong.

Learn how your partner's body receives pleasure and put this knowledge into practice when you make love. Remember that preferences can change over time, so be sure to revisit and renew your lists when necessary.

As well as sensitivity to touch, smell and taste can also be affected in the sexual side of the relationship. I have worked with AS partners, in particular AS women, who find their partners' bodily fluids repulsive and find oral sex, or even in some cases kissing, almost impossible. Sometimes the problem can be remedied if their partner cleans their teeth or has baths. It is something that needs discussion and experimentation in an effort to find a compromise without it becoming confrontational. Confrontation could result in non-disclosure and an avoidance of sex altogether. Sex is about pleasing one another, and caring partners would not want to put their loved ones through something they clearly did not enjoy. It is important to find out what affects the AS partner and to avoid making them feel guilty for being affected by sensory sensitivity.

I have put together a list of the most common effects below. I call them 'passion reducers' as for some individuals that is exactly the effect they have. Read through the list together and identify any that the AS partner is affected by. Some of the issues on the list are of a very sensitive nature and can be quite difficult to discuss, especially in the early stages of a relationship. If it is felt that these issues are too embarrassing or sensitive to talk about alone together, then try to find a psychosexual therapist to discuss them with. Be sure to find someone who is familiar with both autism and the effect of sensory sensitivity on the sexual side of an AS/NT relationship.

▬ Instructions for the AS partner to complete the Passion Reducers List

1. Read through the list below.

2. Tick or circle the areas that affect you in a negative way.

3. On completion, share with your partner.

4. Discuss together ways that you might reduce or eliminate any irritating factors in the environment that might interfere with your sex life.

The Passion Reducers List

Visual distractions
> Having lights on that are too bright
> The room being too dark
> Having light shining through a gap in the curtains/blinds
> Standby lights – television/recorder/mobile phone

Auditory irritations
> Having the television/radio or any noise on in the background, including romantic music
> Clocks ticking
> Whispering or breathing directly into one's ear
> Mobile phone alerts/ringing

Smells that can be off-putting or repulsive
> Specific perfumes, aftershave, body lotion, body spray, deodorant
> Air fresheners, scented candles, oil burners
> Bodily smells
> Breath odour

Tastes that can be unpleasant or nauseating
> Lipstick
> Body lotions/soaps
> Face cream
> Bodily fluids

Touch that is uncomfortable and irritating
> Bed linen
> Nightwear
> Hair
> Finger and toe nails
> Sensitive parts of the body
> Types of touch

On completion of the list, share with your partner and discuss how you can work together to reduce or eliminate these distractions or irritations from your sex life.

Finding a new way of sexual communication

Experimentation and the ability to discuss the sexual side of the relationship openly are important. This might be quite difficult for some partners, especially if using sexual language and terms is something a couple are not used to or feel uncomfortable with. Finding a substitute name for a sexual part of the body can really make a difference as it allows a couple to discuss parts of their bodies as though in the third person. For example, both the vagina and the penis could be personalized with names such as Daisy and Dennis. It might feel easier to say 'Daisy is fast asleep and doesn't think she can wake up tonight' as opposed to 'Sorry, but I am far too tired to make love tonight.' Or it could work to say, 'Dennis has fallen asleep after a long day.' A sense of fun can develop from this. One partner could touch the other and say, 'Oh, Dennis is feeling a bit frisky tonight!'

The aim is to bring fun into sex. This is something that seems to get lost in some AS/NT relationships, often due to not knowing what to say for fear of getting it wrong or hurting the other's feelings. Using pet names and giving sexual parts personalities can avoid communication taking on a personal or clinical tone. It also allows couples to find out whether their partner wants to make love or wants to be close, but not necessarily have an orgasm. For example, a partner could ask whether Daisy wants to come out to play. To which the answer might be: 'Daisy would love Dennis to visit but he's not to worry about making her come.'

This method of communication is not restricted to heterosexual couples and could be easily applied to lesbian or gay couples too, as can all the worksheets in this workbook.

A whole new language can develop between the couple. Pet names can be given for other parts of the body too, such as the breasts and testicles. It is creative and can make sex fun, imaginative and playful. Once again, this will not work for every couple, but when it does work it seems to work well. Decide together if you feel it will work for you. Experiment, choose names, explore with the language you use. Sex should be both a physical pleasure and fun. It should be unrestricted while maintaining respect and trust. Find what works for you. Your sex life is an important part of your relationship as a couple. Maybe think back to how it used to be when you first met. It is sad that for some couples the fun and intimate closeness are lost in time. This can be due to changes in the roles of the couple, from partner to parent, or even step-parent.

Chapter 9

PARENTING

AS well as being a part of a couple, the AS partner is very often a parent too. This brings a new set of variables to the couple's life together. Being a parent is not easy at the best of times, and being a parent affected by autism can be even more difficult. An AS parent will struggle with a child's differing stages of development and the way children constantly change. If there is more than one child, this will mean being aware of multiple differences in ability and the understanding of each child's developmental level.

An example I use to highlight this is a seven-year-old girl who asked her AS dad to help her with some arithmetic homework. Dad was pleased. Being an accountant meant this was his forte. However, instead of dealing with the arithmetic in hand, he took it upon himself to try and teach his daughter some very complex equations he believed would help her understand arithmetic better. It was not long before the girl was in tears and he was frustrated. For her, the equations were beyond her stage of learning. He didn't realize she was too young to grasp such equations. When the mother became involved, it turned into a row between the couple. The upshot of it all was that the very upset little girl did not ask for her father's help again.

What happened relates to lack of theory of mind on the father's part, as his expectations of his daughter's cognitive capacity were far beyond her ability. He did not understand that the developmental stage for her age was very different from how his own brain worked and learned. He did not intend to upset his daughter and was probably at a loss as to why she had become upset. He then felt he had got it wrong, or was being unfairly got at, when his intentions were to help his daughter.

Incidents like this occur in many different forms; it may be at the dinner table over table manners and etiquette, where expectations may be far above what the child is capable of. Dropping crumbs, keeping clothes clean or not making a mess are all potential risk situations. The AS parent may become irritated and frustrated with the child for dropping a drink on the floor, and their reaction may sometimes be out of proportion to the extent of the accident.

Being distracted

Another fraught area that has been raised by the NT parent is fear of the AS parent becoming distracted or not seeing the potential consequences of their behaviour. Examples of this include accounts of children being left alone because the AS parent had become distracted by something they saw as being more important. The AS partner isn't being neglectful, they simply falsely assume the child is more developed than he/she is and is able to manage alone for a short time.

A couple related the following story to me. Before leaving for work, the NT parent asked their AS partner to pick up a prescription from the chemist. The AS partner only remembered this about 15 minutes before the chemist was due to close. By the time the two children had been dressed and strapped into their car seats, they would have been too late for the chemist. Rather than let their partner down and maybe have a confrontation, the AS partner left the children watching television and dashed out to the shop. Meanwhile, the NT parent returned to find the six- and four-year-old alone and distressed. The NT parent was furious with their partner on their return. Tempers flared and many hurtful things were said. The AS partner had not anticipated the consequences both to themselves and to the children.

Occurrences such as these will undermine the trust of the NT parent in their partner's capacity to take care of the children. This can affect the whole family structure and it is likely that the NT parent will become very protective and defensive of the children, resulting in the AS parent feeling isolated and criticized. Some AS parents decide not to be involved with their children's upbringing and distance themselves from the family. They may decide not to take part in any of the decisions involving the childcare and leave the NT parent with total responsibility for the children. This distancing works for some couples, but for the majority of couples, where trust does break down, the AS parent is left feeling on the outside and rejected, while the NT parent feels abandoned by the AS partner's apparent irresponsibility. This will not create a happy environment in which to bring up the children.

When I am working with parents affected by autism, I teach them about their children and specific rules that can never be broken under any circumstances. One aspect of this teaching is to educate regarding how a child develops and what might be expected at specific ages. There is much written about this and plenty of information on the internet. Although development does not always follow a strict process, it is a rough guide as to what a child may or may not be capable of.

Understanding the kids

Learning about their child's developmental stages can encourage better understanding for the AS parent. Liane Holliday Willey (2000) talks about this in a video presentation with Professor Tony Attwood. Liane describes how she came to realize that she did not understand her neurotypical children. She decided that she needed to do something about this in order to provide the best care she could. Liane read books about neurotypical children. Her descriptions are very much the same as what a neurotypical parent might do if their children are affected by autism. It is about learning what the differences are and working with them rather than against them.

House rules

Another worthwhile strategy for maintaining family harmony is to put together a list of house rules. This can be done between the couple or, if the children are old enough, with the whole family. If rules are agreed on and made known, then everyone will know what they are doing and misunderstandings may be avoided. It is important that all should have a fair say in what the house rules are to be, and they should be agreed between the couple or with the children if applicable.

To keep this fair, I recommend that each family member involved has a piece of paper and pen to compile their own personal list of the house rules that would be important to them. Once everyone has completed their list, the family should come together and compare and negotiate what the important rules will be. This will require compromise by everyone. If the children are too young or not able to decide for themselves, then it may be more appropriate if the parents or caregivers do this without involving the children.

WORKSHEET

Example of a List of House Rules

House rules for the Smith family	
Everyone	If it is your mess, then you clean it up.
Everyone	If someone is talking, then do not interrupt.
Oliver and Charlotte	Bedtime is 9pm.
Everyone	Clothes to be washed must be put in the laundry basket.
Oliver	The hamster cage will be cleaned every Saturday.
Oliver and Charlotte	The television will remain off until homework is finished.
Dad	The dog is taken for a walk every evening.
Mum	Don't give tasks to do or expect a conversation when an important football match is on (unless urgent).

▬ Instructions for making a list together of your family's house rules

1. Arrange a time that all the family can be sat together around a table if possible.

2. Give at least 24 hours' notice for this.

3. Ask each family member to think about the house rules they would like to see in place and to whom the house rule should apply.

4. Each person should bring their prepared list to the meeting.

5. Each person should be allowed to take it in turns to read their list to the rest of the family (no more than five minutes).

6. There should be a vote on which rules are to be accepted (aim for an overall total of ten rules).

7. If it is a draw, discuss how the rule might be reapplied to suit all concerned.

8. If the children are too young to participate, the couple can choose five rules each.

9. The rules should be reasonable and all offer some benefit to the family.

10. Don't include any silly or over-controlling rules like 'Dad should always give me a lift' or 'The children will never leave any of their dinner.'

WORKSHEET

List of House Rules

House rules for the . . . . family	

Sharing responsibilities

Some NT parents, when referring to their partner, will tell me that they feel as if they are looking after an extra child, that they are taking responsibility for the whole relationship and family. In my research (Aston 2003a), I found that many NT partners were originally attracted to the childlike qualities they sensed in their partners. For many, this was very appealing in the early stages of the relationship. However, what they found as the relationship progressed was that their partner never emotionally grew up and remained a bit of a 'Peter Pan'.

It may not have been until the children were born that this was noticed. Instead of having a partner sharing the practical and emotional responsibilities of bringing up children, they have a partner who is competing for their attention, as a child sibling might do. In fact, sibling rivalry is an appropriate term in some cases. Again, this is due to not being able to perceive a child's developmental level, or that the relationship their partner has with their child is different and cannot be competed with. This may be difficult for the couple to resolve and may be an issue best addressed with a therapist who has an understanding of the effect of being in an AS family.

Favouritism

Another relevant aspect that can evolve within neurodiverse families is that the AS parent may develop a strong and noticeable preference for one of the children to the exclusion of the others. This can cause many issues, especially for the children who are not favoured, and will need addressing, as it can be a strong precursor for sibling rivalry.

There may be times when the NT parent finds themselves trying to compensate for the less favoured children or becoming overprotective of their feelings. This can be very difficult for families to resolve alone and help may be needed from a well-informed family therapist.

Exploration of why this preference has occurred can help bring the cause out into the open. More often, the reason is due to the AS adult feeling they can relate strongly to one particular child, although that does not mean it is necessarily a child who is also on the autistic spectrum. It is more likely to be the child who shares similar interests to them, and because of their knowledge the AS parent feels more relevant and liked by this son/daughter. Sharing a special interest is a vital ingredient for an individual on the spectrum, and it could be anything from an aptitude for mathematics to an interest in aquatic fish.

• Chapter 10 •

HOME LIFE

Special interests

It is unlikely that the home life of the family is not in some way affected by the AS partner's special interest. It can be an area where the AS partner may be able to contribute to the family, as it is likely they are an expert on their particular interest. Interests can vary and change over time – they can be work related, such as information technology (IT), aircraft or accounting, or hobbies such as PlayStation games, clocks or stamps. Special interests can include anything that the AS person expends much time on and tends to be knowledgeable about. Having a special interest is very important to the person with autism as it can be said to be mood altering. I have learned from my research and from my many AS clients that people with autism have highly active brains, active to the point where switching their brain off from thinking mode and sometimes hyperactivity can be a problem. Many AS clients struggle with sleepless nights, waking up early and just lying in bed constantly churning thoughts over and over.

A special interest is an excellent form of distraction and a way of chilling out. It allows the AS brain to focus and become absorbed in something that is stimulating and pleasurable. It is the AS person's way of relaxing, just as the NT partner may call up a friend or go down to the local pub with some friends to watch a match. I have found that an individual on the spectrum can rapidly become depressed, despondent and feel without purpose when they do not have a special interest.

For most couples, the AS partner's special interest is not a problem. However, it does seem to become a problem when it appears to take over the AS partner's life and conversation. It is then that the NT partner, and probably the rest of the family too, starts to feel neglected and secondary to the special interest. If the interest is outside work, say politics for example, then the NT partner may feel they are living with a workaholic. Let's say that politics is the special interest outside work. The NT partner may find that their AS partner is continually reading about the subject, talking about it, looking it up on the internet or going out campaigning.

This change of interest from their NT partner to something which does not even include them can feel very confusing for the NT partner. It is likely that, initially in the relationship, the NT partner was the special interest and there may have been a time when they were endowed with attention, gifts and, most importantly, their partner's time. For a while, the NT partner felt top of the priority list. Unfortunately, this can all change quite quickly once the relationship is established, particularly when the couple live together, as described in the case study below.

● CASE STUDY: PAUL AND ELAINE

Paul (aged 42) and Elaine (aged 35) met on a bikers' dating site. Although Elaine was quite a novice at motorcycling, she had always wanted to learn to ride and was very pleased when after two attempts she passed her test. Paul, however, had had a total passion for motorbikes for as long as he could remember; as a child he could name on sight the make and model of every conceivable motorcycle ever manufactured. Even more astonishing to his parents, he could name the make and model of a bike purely by the sound of its engine.

Within a matter of weeks, Paul and Elaine embarked on a relationship. Elaine was very flattered by the amount of attention and gifts Paul bestowed on her. She would wake up in the morning to a phone full of compliments and thoughtful messages, he took photos of her wherever they went and constantly proclaimed his love for her. He also bought her gifts that she could never have imagined, including a gold frame in the shape of a motorbike with a photograph of the two of them smiling from within. The list was endless, and needless to say Paul proposed within three months; within nine months they were married and had moved in together.

Elaine came to see me a year later, distraught, unhappy, confused and bewildered – feeling very different from how she described she had felt when she first agreed to marry Paul. Elaine said that she realized something was amiss shortly after they returned from their honeymoon. The honeymoon was riding Route 66 together and Elaine said it had been an amazing experience, although Paul had spent far more time eyeing up the other bikes on the tour and talking with other bikers about bikes than he had with her. Elaine tried to overlook this and join in with Paul's enthusiasm as much as she could. She didn't want anything to spoil their special time together. However, when they returned home Elaine found herself fighting for Paul's attention. He was now spending most of his free time out on his bike, working on his bike, cleaning his bike, reading and researching bikes or talking to his friends about bikes. Elaine had almost stopped going out on her own bike as she now resented everything to do with bikes and consequently felt that going out on her bike was just going to encourage Paul even more.

Elaine had heard about autism and came to therapy saying it was the only thing that made sense of Paul's behaviour. She said she knew Paul loved her, because he had told her so and she knew he wouldn't lie; however, she felt totally unloved because she considered herself to be placed at the bottom of his priority list and all he cared about was his motorbike and all the biking events he attended. Elaine said she felt as though she was going totally mad as Paul just didn't get it, didn't get why she was unhappy and why she begrudged his time spent on his bike. Elaine added that she very much wanted children with Paul but feared she would be bringing them up alone if things did not change between them.

I suggested to Elaine that both she and Paul came to see me together, if Paul was willing, and the following week both attended the session. Over the sessions that followed it became quite evident that Paul was on the spectrum. I explored this with him, and he was not surprised, explaining that his last girlfriend had mentioned it often to him. Elaine was taken back by this as Paul had never mentioned it before, to which he informed her that she had never asked, so why would he? I explored with Paul the idea of being assessed and he said he would give it some thought and do some research.

Paul did his research, and although he didn't believe he needed a formal diagnosis, he agreed as he felt it would help them both to be certain. After Paul had been formally diagnosed, we continued our work together and put together schedules, rules and timetables that were equally fair to both. Paul came to understand that Elaine, just like his bike, needed regular TLC (tender loving care), and once he understood what that meant in terms of their relationship and knew what was required of him, he was more than happy to oblige. Elaine made an effort to ensure that her needs were met; she had a good support group and took time out for herself, joined a women's walking group and looked forward to motherhood.

As with Paul and Elaine, there are definite times when, if a special interest takes over the relationship, strategies and mechanisms need to be brought into place for the couple.

Setting time limits can help. However, these need to be discussed and decided between the couple so that it is fair for both of them. If both have interests then it is even easier to work out a balance in the relationship that allows both to allocate time to enjoy their interests. If the NT partner does not have a specific interest, spending time with friends in an AS-free environment where communication can flow on a more emotional level can be beneficial and satisfying.

Making a written timetable, so that it can be referred to, is better than just relying on verbal agreements. If the timetable is agreed by both, then it becomes a type of contract and will reinforce the fact that both need to adhere to it. Not only will the timetable allow each partner time alone, it will also set aside that quality time together that is crucial in feeding the relationship and increasing the bond the couple share together. Finding an interest both partners like is not always easy. Some of the ones that clients have found to work are board or card games, music, theatre, cinema, motorcycling, cycling, running, walking, going to the gym, water sports and visiting historical sites. This shared interest may appeal for very different reasons. The NT partner might find, for example, that a historical building allows them to capture a glimpse of the past or romanticize about the lives of historical figures, while the AS partner may be enthralled by the architecture, its intricacy or the sheer enormity of the building.

Often, shared interests are those that do not involve too much communication; certainly, motorcycling, theatre, water sports or even running can be enjoyed without having to talk. The only discussion might be after the event in direct reference to the interest in question, which usually suits both partners.

Time awareness

In my research, I have found that AS individuals are either ruled rigidly by the clock or have no awareness of time at all. Both of these characteristics can cause difficulties with family life, and the NT partner may find they are either being dominated by a time schedule or constantly being let down by their partner's apparent inability to arrive anywhere on time, whether that be meeting for a social event, collecting the children from school or arriving on time for a parents' meeting.

If the AS partner has a history of being late or forgetting to turn up to appointments, the NT partner will find they are taking on more and more responsibilities as the feeling they can trust their partner to do things on time diminishes. With the balance of responsibilities weighing heavily on the NT partner, feelings of being alone and being the carer for everyone, including their partner, will lead to pebbles being added to their bucket. If the AS partner is willing, there are strategies that can be put into place to help bring some change to this situation. Even with these changes, the NT partner, as social guide in the relationship, will still be carrying the majority of responsibilities for family life, regardless of whether they are male or female.

Dominated by time

Some people affected by autism may find comfort and safety in being able to control their environment by developing time-related routines. For example, they may insist on the evening meal being served at exactly 6pm. Unfortunately, once established, this rule will become inflexible with no exceptions for other family members being proffered. Imposing these routines on their partner and family is a form of domestic abuse and is unacceptable. An AS partner may not appreciate how much their routines impinge detrimentally on their partner and children. They may need to hear this from a third party.

When there are children in the relationship, the AS partner can become draconian with their routines in an effort to control the children, whom the AS partner is already struggling to understand or relate to. In some cases, when the AS partner realizes this, there will be an effort to change or the NT partner may decide that they are simply not going to be controlled in this way anymore and will be learning to say no.

My advice to couples is, if possible, not to allow routines such as these to establish themselves in the first place. The longer a routine is exercised, the harder it will be to change.

No time awareness

On the other side of the coin, some NT partners describe how their partner just does not seem to be able to organize events or make plans regardless of how much they encourage them. This is especially for anything time related, and the AS partner will struggle to figure out how long it will take to get ready or to incorporate into the schedule the time it will take to arrive somewhere. The only exception to this seems to be when an event is something the AS partner is interested in, for example a football match involving their favourite team. In that case, they will know exactly what time kick-off is and be ready for it. A useful strategy then is to find a link with their interest and the timing of an important event such as a parents' meeting. This could be achieved by saying 'It will take you until half-time to get to the school meeting' or 'It will take you the length of the 10 o'clock news to get to the school meeting.' It is very likely that the AS partner will have a mental record of how long their favourite things take, if only to ensure they set aside the time to enjoy them.

Discuss together what you could use to make this work. I have set out an example of a Time Awareness Sheet on the following page and there is a blank one for you both to fill in together.

WORKSHEET

Example of a Time Awareness Sheet

Task	Time to allow
Driving from work to the school.	Favourite programme on Radio 4.
We have to leave in 30 minutes.	An episode of *EastEnders*.
Driving from home to the school.	Rugby match half-time.
Meeting me in an hour and three-quarters.	Football match full time.
Driving to pick Sally up from her martial arts class.	Running two miles.
Driving to pick Johnny up from his piano class.	Walking the dog.
I will meet you back here in one hour.	A yoga class.
Get the dinner out of the oven in 40 minutes.	A workout in the gym.

▬ Instructions for filling in the Time Awareness Sheet

1. Arrange some quiet time to sit down together to identify relevant tasks.

2. Write a list in the left-hand column on the time sheet.

3. The NT partner will have to identify how much time needs to be allocated to these tasks.

4. Explore together an activity that the AS partner is interested in that takes a similar amount of time to complete, listen to or watch.

5. The NT partner will need to learn to use these representations when arranging with their partner to carry out tasks that are time dependent.

WORKSHEET
Time Awareness Sheet

Task	Time to allow

Selective hearing

It is not uncommon for the NT partner to describe how their AS partner seemingly gets stuck on a minor aspect of a discussion. Sometimes the AS partner may say that, in retrospect, they can see they had become stuck on something and should have let it go. However, this does not seem to prevent it from reoccurring when a new situation presents itself. Once this happens, the discussion breaks down and can turn into an argument. The NT partner may suggest that their partner has selective hearing, that is, picks out from a discussion the bits they want to hear and deliberately ignores the rest. In a sense this is correct. However, it is not deliberate, and for many AS individuals it can be due to their perception of being criticized.

For example, a female NT partner might come in one day from having visited a friend and say, 'Janet showed me the new bathroom her John has just fitted. It's really lovely and makes me wonder about getting an estimate on having ours done.' Innocuous enough, one might say, but the male AS partner may have heard criticism in the first sentence, insofar as she is saying he doesn't do things like that. In the second sentence, where she suggests having the bathroom done by someone professional, he may think she is saying that he is not as capable as John, and an argument ensues.

These situations are very difficult to predict and very difficult to diffuse. Our NT partner will not understand why their comment caused so much resentment. If the situation is to be diffused, the NT partner needs to remember that this is selective hearing, it is not deliberate. The onus is on them to pause and try and find out what criticism their AS partner thinks they heard.

Getting the priorities right

AS people often have difficulties in seeing what is or is not important and can become fixated on a trivial or minor task. They may have no idea how to prioritize tasks and refuse to leave a job until it is completed, much to the frustration of those around them who may be trying to have more important tasks completed first.

For example, the AS partner has decided to build a made-to-measure bookcase for their book collection. This is no small task, but the AS partner is skilful and determined to give it as much attention and time as possible, as all the books will need to fit neatly into place. Meanwhile, the NT partner has returned home having bought a couple of shrubs for the garden. The NT partner finds it difficult to dig such deep holes alone and asks for their partner to help. The AS partner, totally engrossed, simply says, 'You'll have to wait till I have finished the bookcase!' The NT partner tries to explain that the shrubs need to be planted and it won't take too long. Both partners are now upset, and both are seeing it from different perspectives. The NT partner is aggrieved as they feel they work really hard to make the garden nice for both of them. The AS partner is annoyed as they now believe their partner resents the building of the bookcase.

With the difficulty in applying theory of mind, the AS partner is not able to see the importance to their partner of planting the shrubs. They cannot see that the task will not take too long in comparison to the bookcase, which is becoming a long-term project.

The other side of this is that an AS partner may struggle to prioritize a series of tasks. This can result in them becoming completely overwhelmed at the very thought of the volume of tasks to be achieved and consequently not manage to accomplish any. They may attempt to begin a task but then become distracted and start another and another, until utter chaos develops. At this point, the AS partner may walk away and leave everyone else with the job of clearing up.

The central executive area within the brain governs organizational skills. This is explained very well in Tony Attwood's excellent, well-researched book *The Complete Guide to Asperger's Syndrome* (2007). I highly recommend this book to anyone whose life is affected by autism. Difficulties within this area of the brain can cause problems in prioritizing tasks.

It may sometimes seem that priority is often given to those tasks the AS person wants to do most, rather than those that are most important. One way to help prioritize tasks is by making a list and using colours to illuminate the importance of the tasks in question. A whiteboard or large piece of paper can be divided into two lists, one written in red and one written in green.

Example of Organizing Priorities Sheet

High priority (red)	Low priority (green)
Roger to: fix leaking tap in the bathroom	Both to: clean out fishpond
Roger to: replace inner tube on Johnny's bike	Roger to: prune the apple tree
Mary to: get a present for Mum's birthday	Mary to: sort out drawers in bedroom
Mary to: take faulty radio back to shop	Both to: choose a new bed together
Both to: go to the travel agents to arrange summer holiday	Roger to: take coat into cleaners
	Mary to: make a dental appointment for Johnny

▬ Instructions for filling in the Organizing Priorities Sheet

1. Arrange a time when you can sit down together and not be disturbed.

2. Both think about the tasks you need to do.

3. Arrange together which should be given the highest priority.

4. Arrange who is going to do the task or if it is something for both to do.

5. No more than two tasks each plus two tasks for both can be entered on the red side at any time.

6. Write the list down on a whiteboard or large piece of paper.

7. Put this up somewhere prominent.

8. As a task from the red side is completed then a task from the green side can be transferred over to the red. It will then become a red task.

9. Tasks on the red side must always take priority over the green list.

Organizing Priorities Sheet

High priority (red)	Low priority (green)

As with any of the worksheets in this book, the couple should experiment to discover what works for them. It is hoped that new ways of communicating and sharing time as a couple and a family will develop, as understanding increases and matures between the couple, not just for now but for their future time together.

Chapter 11

THE FOUR STUMBLING BLOCKS

ALTHOUGH all AS/NT relationships will be different, there will four stumbling blocks that will, because of the neurological differences between the couple, present themselves in the majority of AS/NT relationships.

These blocks are: lack of emotional support, saying the wrong thing, self-absorbed and not self-aware, and an overreaction to any perceived criticism. I call these blocks because they really do get in the way of the smooth running of the relationship and it can feel that they constantly rear their ugly heads in a way that is frustratingly repetitive, especially for the NT partner. I will deal with these four stumbling blocks one by one, although they are all entwined together, as will be shown.

Lack of emotional support

Studies on theory of mind have revealed that empathy encompasses more than one major factor – a cognitive factor and an affective factor (Bird *et al.* 2010). Affective empathy is the ability to feel and share another's emotions, while cognitive empathy is the ability to read the emotions of another and to separate that feeling from our own, recognizing the distinction between the feelings of ourselves and another. Putting the two together will result in the ability to be able to interpret, understand and feel the emotions of another person without confusing their feelings with our own. This is crucial when in a close relationship as it allows automatic and spontaneous empathy, which is critical to the smooth running of that relationship. Research is finding that individuals on the spectrum have more difficulty with cognitive empathy than with affective empathy. This very much supports my own beliefs and certainly explains why if an emotional situation which is affecting the NT partner is explained in a clear and logical way, the AS partner can feel and offer empathy.

An underdeveloped theory of mind in individuals on the spectrum will yield an inability to fully and spontaneously empathize, making it difficult to instinctively understand someone else's thoughts, feelings or perspectives (Thompson 2008). An underdeveloped theory of mind underpins what autism fundamentally is. This has been shown in numerous experiments with children on the spectrum, the most famous of which is the Sally–Anne dolls experiment[1] (Baron-Cohen, Leslie and Frith 1985). This experiment indicated that compared to neurotypical children, children affected by autism were not able to put themselves in someone else's mind state and see things through their eyes, not their own. Although, as with most research, this study has come under criticism, this is how I hear the NT partner describe what is happening in their relationship. I hear comments such as 'He just has no idea how I feel', 'She only thinks about herself and seems totally oblivious to how I am feeling!' and 'If I am sick or upset, he just cannot cope, or he just walks away'. Most commonly I hear 'He/she just doesn't get it!'

A lack of spontaneous empathy shown by the AS partner can, understandably, be interpreted as not caring by the NT partner. This can cause misconstructions, arguments and, if not resolved, a complete breakdown in communication, which will be upsetting and disturbing for both in the relationship. I want to accentuate the word 'spontaneous', as I have found that individuals on the milder end of the autistic spectrum are able to empathize with others, providing it is either a situation they can personally relate to or the other person describes their feelings in a clear and logical way. Although explaining how they feel in this way requires time and patience on behalf of the NT partner, as the empathy sought is not offered automatically, it is worth the time and effort. I have found that if an explanation is offered in a non-confrontational way and is logical, the AS partner can come to understand their partner's emotional responses. However, this will not happen spontaneously, and will not happen if the situation is too emotionally charged or feels threatening.

---

1   The Sally–Anne false belief task used a story about two dolls called Sally and Anne to test the level of theory of mind in children with autism.

Unfortunately, an emotional crisis is very likely to be emotionally charged because it is just that, a crisis! A crisis can take many forms: death, loss of employment, friendship or material belongings, an accident or illness, a robbery, internet hacking and scams, the list is endless. All can leave an individual inconsolable, bereft and emotionally needy, and it is often the person's partner who is needed most in these turbulent times.

The AS partner can suddenly find themselves feeling totally lost in a fog of unexpected events and expectations with no instructions or map to tell them what to do, what to say, how to respond and how to behave. Total autistic nightmare! One AS client who was in the military explained it by saying it was like trying to disarm a bomb with a blindfold on.

I cannot stress enough how much the fear of confrontation affects so many AS individuals on the spectrum, and this fear can be immobilizing and inhibiting. Unfortunately, this fear can cause a 'rabbit in the headlights' non-response from the AS partner (see Chapter 5), leaving the NT partner feeling totally alone and forsaken at a time when their need is at its greatest. An example of this is given in the case study below.

● CASE STUDY: JILL AND COLIN

Jill had recently been diagnosed with an underactive thyroid and was finding the juggling act of maintaining work and family very difficult and incredibly tiring. By the end of the day, she felt absolutely spent, and as soon as she sat down, she found herself falling asleep. She had been far from her usual cheery self and could find herself in a flood of tears for no reason at all. Colin had been finding this very stressful and did not know what to do to make Jill happy anymore. She seemed sensitive to everything he said and he had resigned himself to the fact that if he said very little and kept out of Jill's way, he could avoid the risk of upsetting her. Colin spent more and more time on the computer organizing the family accounts or searching for up-to-date research on aerodynamics.

It had been arranged for Jill to attend a hospital appointment for a thyroid scan as there were concerns over a swelling that had been detected on her thyroid gland. Jill had told Colin she had an appointment and was going with her sister; it was arranged for the coming Thursday. The news was not good, and when she arrived home, she was very upset and, not surprisingly, concerned over the results. When Colin came home from work, he found Jill on the phone to her mother sounding very tearful and upset. Rather than going up to her or waiting for her to finish on the phone, he went back into the hall, put his coat back on, called their golden retriever, put on her lead and went straight back out the door. He left his mobile on the hall shelf and did not return for over an hour. When he came in, he informed Jill he had had some fish and chips in the park so didn't need feeding and went into the study to do some research.

Jill was really hurt that Colin had showed no concern for the fact she was upset or why she was upset. She did not go into him, rather she went to bed and cried herself to sleep. Neither talked to each other for days, and it was only because Jill's mother intervened and explained to Colin what had happened at the hospital that he could understand Jill's distress. Colin had wrongly presumed that Jill's distress indicated that it was something he had done, such as not going to the hospital with her, so he had completely distanced himself from her and interpreted her tears and silence as anger.

This example can be likened to many others that, although seemingly all very different, are fundamentally the same. They are all due to difficulty in applying cognitive empathy, which can cause the misreading of others and the misinterpretation of their feelings and behaviour. If Jill had reminded Colin about her appointment or even better called him or sent him a text regarding the results, he would have had time to prepare himself for Jill being upset. When Colin was told what had happened, he was devastated and totally there for Jill, willing to support her in any way she needed, as long as she told him what that was.

Saying the wrong/inappropriate thing!

I could certainly write a book purely on this topic alone and I have yet to encounter an NT partner who hasn't got their own catalogued list of unexpected and sometimes quite hard-hitting remarks that have been delivered to them by their partner. An important point to make here is that it is rarely the AS partner's intention to hurt their partner, and the majority of remarks that are made are the consequence of total honesty, trying to be funny or simply that they felt their partner needed to know the truth.

In many cases, it is not just the remark that can be hard-hitting, it is also the timing or situation in which the remark is given that makes it a seriously wrong or inappropriate thing to say. For example, one lady asked her AS husband if her bottom looked okay in her leggings, to which he replied, 'Yes, your bottom is fine for an older woman; a bit of toning up might help.' Her husband was being totally honest and was quite shocked when his wife removed the leggings and threw them at him!

These remarks frequently occur in stressful or emotional situations. This links in to the first stumbling block – *lack of emotional support* – especially in a crisis situation. Crisis moments are rarely predictable and there is no time to rehearse or prepare a script. Everything becomes dependent on spontaneity, which requires a fully working theory of mind and the ability to read the emotions and reactions of everyone around at the time. Finding themselves in the middle of the chaos caused by an unpredicted event is not the best environment for our AS partner to be in, and without a prepared script they will often say the first thing that comes to them. It is at times like this that a pause button would be useful or, more appropriate, a replay button as most of my AS clients would dearly love to be able to turn the clock back and edit out the remark that they made.

The other reaction to crisis and emotional situations that has an impact on the NT partner is the AS partner who will try to fix an emotional crisis by saying the first thing that comes to mind. Unfortunately, this is rarely the most appropriate statement to make and can quickly exacerbate the situation. It is rarely the AS partner's intention to say the wrong thing, and the reply they give is often said in total honesty; however, there are times when total honesty becomes brutal honesty and can do more harm than good.

To be able to work out what is the best and most supportive thing to say to someone, especially when they are emotional, requires the ability to be able to put oneself into the emotional mind state of the other and see it from their perspective. To do this requires a fully developed theory of mind and a total absence of alexithymia.

Many of the comments I have heard over the years are said without thought of how they may be heard. Many of the statements that are said are probably thoughts that would pass through the mind of a non-AS partner, but they would not be said out loud. For example, one NT partner explained to me how on their holiday their partner would point out how attractive some of the women were on the beach, when at the time she was struggling with her weight after the birth of their first child. All the women he admiringly referred to were very slim and of course she found this really hurtful, but when it was mentioned to him, he was really surprised as he had presumed his wife would find them attractive too as she had said she hoped to be slim again soon.

Saying the wrong thing can also occur when the AS partner attempts to make light of an emotional situation or how their partner feels. This is often by trying to joke about it, which rarely works out, as often the joke can unintentionally appear very insensitive. The following case study provides an example of this.

● CASE STUDY: MARGARET AND BEN

Margaret had had the most horrendous day at work. She had fallen out with one of her work colleagues and felt all the office were gossiping about her. She arrived home at the same time as her partner and burst into tears as soon as they both reached the kitchen.

Ben listened as she told him about her day, but Margaret quickly noticed that he glanced at the clock and so she asked him if she was keeping him from something. Her partner replied honestly to say that the six o'clock news was on and could she wait until the news had finished as, after all, she could leave, as jobs like hers were relatively easy to acquire! Chuckling to himself, he left the room. Unsurprisingly, Margaret was gutted, and her reaction to this was not kind as all her frustration and pain erupted and was vented towards Ben before she finally ran upstairs and locked herself in the bathroom. Meanwhile, Ben was left feeling totally confused and did not know what he had done wrong, so made himself a cup of tea and sat down to watch the rest of the news. Eventually, Margaret came back downstairs and apologized for her outburst. She had expected that Ben would apologize too and ask her to continue to tell him about her awful day. Of course, he didn't and resumed watching the news, feeling pleased that Margaret had apologized for her behaviour.

Ben had been diagnosed as being on the spectrum only six months earlier and both were attending couple therapy. This was Margaret's saving grace as she was able to recognize what had transpired and decided to wait until the next day when they went to therapy and explain it there. The therapist understood how Margaret must have felt and was able to explain to Ben in an objective and unemotional way what he should have done and said. They also spent time discussing priorities as Ben could have watched the news when it was repeated at seven o'clock. Ben was encouraged and supported to learn more about his condition and together they put strategies in place for the future.

This couple were fortunate to have a good enough therapist who understood the dynamics of neurodiverse relationships and even more fortunate that Margaret had a good understanding of the effects of being on the spectrum. This example also shows how Ben's lack of self-awareness had prevented him from gathering enough insight to see into how his actions had impacted on Margaret. Ben could only see that he had had the best of intentions and felt Margaret was being oversensitive and emotional. Unfortunately, this can become a reoccurring issue for couples and is once again linked to theory of mind and exacerbated by the presence of alexithymia.

Self-absorbed and not self-aware

The third stumbling block is lack of self-awareness and it does appear in many cases where the AS partner is often not aware of how the things they say or do impact on their partner. For instance, in the case of Margaret and Ben, Ben was not aware of how his joke and walking out had impacted on Margaret and caused her to become angry with him. He could only see that she had been angry with him and that had hurt him. Self-absorbed and not self-aware, Ben was so busy feeling his own pain he had totally missed how his words and actions had caused Margaret pain, and that is what made her angry.

Research has found that self-awareness is an essential component when applying empathy. If an individual is not aware or able to identify their own feelings, it is particularly difficult to identify how others feel (Decety and Jackson 2004). The way this appears to show itself in a relationship is an apparent lack of awareness of how the words or behaviour of the AS partner impact on the NT partner. The AS partner is often only aware of the reaction they observe and how it impacts on them and completely miss the link between what they said or did to provoke the reaction in their partner. Here is a case study that helps to explain this.

● CASE STUDY: SHELLY AND ALICE

Shelly and Alice were a young lesbian couple in their thirties, who had been in a civil partnership for five years. Alice had been diagnosed with autism when she was 15, and worked as a successful surgeon for a university hospital. Shelly worked as a carer in a home for the elderly.

Shelly had been feeling quite down for a few weeks; her mother had had a major stroke and her health had been deteriorating rapidly. It was a Sunday evening, and both were feeling quite exhausted after a long hard week.

Shelly wanted to talk to Alice about her feelings and how it looked far more likely that her mother was not going to survive for much longer. Alice was aware she had an early morning start the next day and was totally absorbed in a book she was reading about the latest developments in laparoscopic and endoscopic surgery, which formed part of her special interests.

Shelly took a cup of tea into the sitting room for them both and sat herself down next to Alice. She started to talk about her feelings regarding her mother, how worried she felt about her mother dying and how she felt she was struggling to cope and did not know what to do. Before long, Shelly had dissolved into a flood of tears.

Alice was quite taken aback at how upset Shelly was, and also a little put out as she had been trying hard to concentrate on the book she was reading as she felt it was important for her work as a surgeon. Alice went straight into the 'fix it quick' mode, saying to Shelly, 'I am really surprised at how you are behaving over this. I would have thought in your job you would be used to old people dying!'

It was now Shelly's turn to be taken aback and become even more upset at how Alice could compare her grief for her mother to the job she did with the elderly.

Alice reacted strongly to this, claiming she was only trying to help and was fed up of the way Shelly had been lately, accusing her of being angry and hostile all the time.

Shelly retaliated by shouting that she was only like this because of what Alice had said, but Alice was not able to make the link between the two as she believed she had genuinely been trying to help Shelly manage better and strongly believed she was the innocent victim of Shelly's anger.

Incidences like the one shared between Shelly and Alice are not uncommon and appear to come out of nowhere at the most unexpected times – usually at times when emotions or crisis situations are being discussed. It can be very difficult to try to explain that comments such as Alice's in the case study, regardless of all the good intentions, are hurtful and inappropriate. Sometimes they have to be heard and explained to a third party, such as a therapist, to get the message across. Confusing being upset and hurt with being angry and hostile is a reoccurring difficulty that is frequently brought by the NT partner into the therapy room. Often the reason is the AS partner's oversensitivity to any comment which they believe could be critical or attacking.

Overreaction to perceived criticism

If an AS individual is struggling to read the more subtle signs of body language and facial expression and has accumulated a history of reading others incorrectly, provoking a negative reaction from them, it is not surprising that the reaction to any perceived criticism is a defensive one. In the excellent book *The Seven Principles for Making Marriage Work* (2000), John Gottman and Nan Silver discuss defensiveness in great detail and highlight it as one of the major causes of relationship breakdown, arguing that it is a person's way of blaming the other person. Defensiveness is a way of not taking responsibility for the issue or problem that has occurred.

Being over and unnecessarily defensive can make any form of good communication impossible, as it will cause a major stumbling block between the couple, making them frustrated and exhausted by trying to get their point across. It is a block that can find its way into all relationships if invited in. In AS/NT relationships it appears to be a permanent lodger for some couples, and the only way of solving the issue is to give this lodger notice to leave!

Defensiveness is a useful reaction if under direct attack for no reason. Unfortunately, in the case of AS partners, it may occur regardless of whether they are under attack, due to misreading the intent and purpose behind the message received. Below is a case study that illustrates this, and it might also be worth revisiting the case study of David and Amy in Chapter 2.

● CASE STUDY: TERRY AND JACKIE

Terry and Jackie were in their sixties and had a large family comprising four children and six grandchildren. It was Jackie's birthday and they were holding a barbeque to celebrate.

Terry had been diagnosed with mild autism and they both had a good understanding of what it meant to their relationship. Terry enjoyed being in charge of the barbeque as he liked to have a role when socializing that he felt confident with. However, the day was not going as well as it could; the weather was somewhat threatening, and the family had arrived early.

Terry felt under pressure to get the barbeque going. He would have preferred to have done this before the family descended on them but realized this was not going to happen on this occasion.

Everyone sat down, chattering and drinking, children playing, and Terry, in his attempt to rush the food, was trying to barbeque sausages, chicken and beef burgers all at the same time. Jackie brought out the plates and, pointing to the sausages, said, 'They look done; shall I take them off the barbeque?' This comment was not meant in any way to undermine Terry or criticize his abilities as a cook. However, what Terry heard was that he was making a mess of this and was obviously in Jackie's eyes incapable of being in charge of the barbeque. He handed the fork to Jackie, took off his apron and said, 'Okay, if that is what you think, get someone else to cook the food.' At this, Terry left the house and didn't return until everyone had left!

Jackie and all the family were very upset, and Jackie could not figure out what on earth it was she had said that had provoked such an extreme reaction.

Scenarios like the one above are plentiful; some are minor and others can escalate into major arguments. Most could be avoided either by the NT partner being more selective and thoughtful with the words used or the AS partner recognizing and accepting that not everything their NT partner says is a form of criticism.

Different from the other chapters in this book, I have no worksheets to offer to solve or fix these four stumbling blocks. The aim of the chapter is to bring them into awareness as they are likely to all have an impact in one way or another on the majority of AS/NT relationships. The only way a couple can work through these stumbling blocks is through accepting that they will happen, understanding why they happen and learning how to lessen their impact. Having a good sense of humour can also make a huge difference to how these issues are perceived. In my work with clients, it is the couples who manage to look back on these difficult and sometimes very hurtful situations and laugh who reach a successful resolution.

Laughter is food for the soul, and couples who can manage this have relationships that are most likely to survive.

Sometimes a couple will feel that they need a helping hand to work through the issues that have arisen in their relationship and they decide to seek the support of a third party such as a couple therapist to help resolve a sensitive issue or to help them get the relationship back on track. Making this decision is very important and needs consideration and planning.

Chapter 12

COUPLE THERAPY

I HAVE been working as a couple therapist since 1994. In 1998, I began to specialize full time in couples affected by autism. Therapists working specifically with AS clients and couples in the nineties were virtually non-existent. Over the past 20 years this has improved greatly as learning and understanding of autism have increased. Now a search on the British Association for Counselling and Psychotherapy (BACP) website under 'Find a therapist' shows there are more and more therapists advertising that they are happy to accept and work with couples when one or both partners are affected by an autistic spectrum condition. However, I do find that the skills therapists offer in this area can be quite diverse.

I have been running workshops for therapists and psychosexual therapists for over 20 years, and in these workshops, I have encountered therapists who show a genuine empathy and understanding of the realities of being in an AS/NT relationship and I feel assured that they will do an excellent job working with couples. Unfortunately, I have also encountered therapists whom I would not recommend working in this area. I have heard many disheartening stories from couples who have felt that their relationships were damaged by therapy due to a total lack of empathy and understanding from the therapist as to what it means to be in a neurologically mixed relationship.

Deciding to go for couple therapy can be an important and sometimes daunting step for a couple and there are many things to consider when choosing a therapist that is right for both of you. In this chapter, I discuss some important factors to consider when choosing to go for therapy. Work through this together and take from it the points that are important to you both.

Where to look

This will obviously depend on where you live. Using an internet search engine is the most popular way of searching, and most countries will have a site that can be used to search for therapists on. In England, a popular site is the BACP website, although there are many others. In America, Psychology Today: Find a Therapist is quite popular. You might want to find a therapist who shares your faith and there are websites that offer this. Ensure that you use a site that lists only qualified and registered therapists and psychotherapists.

How much will I pay?

Charges for therapy seem to vary greatly according to the level of training and/or expertise of the therapist and where they are located. One important rule is that paying more money will not guarantee you get a better therapist. When I did an online search, I was quite surprised at the wide range of prices that clients were being expected to pay for this service. Unfortunately, there are no guidelines for prices that clients can refer to, and it appears to be totally at the discretion of the therapist to decide what they want to charge. In England, prices vary from £70 to £200 per hour for couple therapy, and others are charging into the thousands to secure a slot of 12 sessions. I do feel that unfortunately some therapists are taking advantage of the limited choice of services available for what are often very desperate couples struggling hard to keep their relationships together.

Do not feel pressurized to spend more than you can afford. As I stated earlier, price does not automatically mean you will see a more suitable therapist, nor will it determine the outcome of the therapy sessions. Therapists are there to guide, educate, support, challenge and offer empathetic understanding of the unique situations their clients need support with. All of this should be automatically offered regardless of the price charged, but this will not guarantee success. Success will depend not only on the therapist but also on the couple's readiness to make changes and, most importantly, the amount of love and commitment that the couple share together.

Where will they be located?

Choose your location carefully as you may be attending for a long time. Think together about how far you both want to travel for therapy. Going to therapy is a big commitment and there are times when you may feel quite exhausted after a session, especially if you have been at work all day. If you are arriving at therapy tired and worn out, you may not be able to focus or retain the learning that develops from it.

What if the therapist knows me or my partner?

Some couples feel they want to see a therapist outside their local area as they are concerned about bumping into them while out or that the therapist might know someone they know. Any therapist worth their salt will quickly raise this issue if they feel that the boundaries are compromised in any way and will inform you of the situation and may refer you elsewhere. It is important for a therapist to not have any prior knowledge of you or your family, where you work, or any information that you have not given them.

All therapists should adhere to a strict code of ethics. Ensuring client confidentiality is an essential criterion and is necessary for client trust. For this reason, therapists should always keep their client's confidence with the exception of legal or ethical situations where the therapist may be obliged to break confidentiality. (Legally therapists are obliged to break confidentiality if a client discloses acts of terrorism and money laundering or if they are summoned by a court of law to do so. Ethically, therapists also have a duty of care and may have to break confidentiality if they feel their client or another is at risk of harm.) The only person that your case will be discussed with will be the therapist's supervisor, and this should be carried out without revealing any personal or recognizable details of the clients. The supervisor will also be governed by the same ethical rules of confidentiality.

What to look for in a therapist

Consider together the bullet points below:

- Do you want to see a therapist who has personal experience of autism?

- Do you want to see a therapist who has attended courses or workshops on autism?

- Do either of you have a preference for a male or a female therapist?

- Do you want to see a therapist who is in a specific age group?

- Do you want to see a therapist who understands heterosexual, gay, lesbian, transgender or transsexual clients?

- Do you want to see a therapist who understands the culture or country you come from?

- If you are living in a country where the language is not your first language, then do you want to see a therapist who speaks your first language?

- Do you want to see a therapist who shares your faith?

Some of the above may be very important to you; however, if you are both going to therapy over issues in your relationship that you both believe are related to the fact that one, or both, of you is on the spectrum, then this should take priority. You could find the most perfectly matched therapist out there, but if they have no understanding of the dynamics of a neurologically mixed relationship then they will not be able to offer the understanding, education and support you both require.

Qualifications/training

As you are going as a couple, it is very important that your therapist is fully qualified to work with couples. I am aware that some therapists advertise as being couple therapists after only attending a one- or two-day course. I do not feel such a short course is adequate. My own training was with Relate and took five years of intense teaching and personal development. Working with couples requires the capacity to have a full and deep understanding of the subtleties and the interactive intimate relationship that is shared by the couple. Every couple is different, and sometimes the dynamics that govern the relationship can be both ambiguous and obscure. It will take time, intuition and insight to be able to dig deep and bring the bones of the relationship out into the open, to be explored and enriched.

If a therapist is working with a neurologically mixed couple then they are working with two very different and sometimes opposing agendas, thought processes, needs, expectations and perspectives. A therapist can only do this if they have a deep knowledge and understanding of both people in the relationship and can work professionally as an interpreter and educator between the two.

When do you want to go to couple therapy?

Both ask yourselves – why now? What has made one of you or both of you decide to seek therapy now? Unfortunately, for many the decision is made too late, when the relationship has reached its lowest point. Therapy is then sought as a last chance, a last hope for the relationship. The couple are emotionally and physically exhausted, tired and ready to give up and separate. This can make it very hard for the therapist, especially if one partner has made the decision to separate and the other wishes to try again and continue. Be honest when you go to therapy so that the therapist knows exactly what each of you is hoping for.

How long will the sessions last?

Most therapists offer a 50-minute session. However, I have found in my own experience that 50 minutes is not long enough for couples when you put autism into the equation. Processing sensitive and emotional information for most of my AS clients requires longer than a 50-minute session. I have found that one-and-a half hours or two hours suits couples better and works well. Equally, spacing these sessions out to every other week rather than every week allows clients more time to process and digest the experience together.

One week is not always enough time for couples to put into action the strategies and learning from the sessions and a two-week time period works better. Explore possibilities and availability with your chosen therapist to work out together what will best suit your needs and your therapist's options.

How long do you want to go to couple therapy for?

Are you looking for short-term or long-term therapy? This can make a difference to the type of therapist you choose. Psychotherapy tends to take longer and be more drawn out. A therapist who focuses more on cognitive behavioural therapy (CBT) in their approach may offer short-term therapy. Discuss this at the start of therapy to ensure that your therapist can offer the type and length of therapy you are hoping for.

Much of my work is based on education, as the issues that arise between couples are often due to a misconstrued view or lack of understanding of the following:

- What it means to be on the spectrum.

- What is due to being on the spectrum.

- What is caused by personality.

- What can be changed or not changed.

- How being on the spectrum will impact on the relationship.

When working with couples, I am often in the role of interpreter to help them develop a clearer insight into their partner's sometimes very different perspective. So when looking for a therapist, consider what type of therapy they are trained in. Often clients on the spectrum find therapy that takes a more structured or solution-focused approach and involves an amount of psychoeducation more suitable for them. Therapy that is less structured, more emotion focused and dependent on a client's insight into their own difficulties may be too difficult for individuals with AS to work with successfully. This type of therapy can rely heavily on the client's ability for self-reflection and emotional expression, both of which can be difficult for those on the spectrum. For this reason, CBT can often be preferable for AS clients. Finding an integrative therapist can be as good a choice as it means the therapist is trained to combine techniques from a number of therapeutic approaches, allowing them to adapt the style of therapy to best suit the client's needs. Integrative therapists, however, will vary in which approaches they have been trained to combine, so check this first.

Exactly what are you both hoping to gain from therapy?

It is important that a couple have a clear understanding of what they hope to gain from therapy prior to attending, both individually and as a couple. Below I have put together a list of agendas for you both to consider and fill in. Once completed, share with your partner.

▬ Instructions for both partners to complete the Couple Therapy Agenda

1. Choose a time when you are quiet and not likely to be disturbed.

2. Read through the list of possible agendas that you wish to fulfil from therapy.

3. Fill this in separately.

4. Tick the boxes that apply to you.

5. If your own personal agenda is not mentioned, enter this in the empty rows.

6. Share your answers together.

WORKSHEET

Couple Therapy Agenda

	YES	NO
A deeper understanding of autism		
Help in communication		
Strategies and aids		
Exploration of trust issues		
Having an interpreter to help you understand each other		
Help and support over sexual/intimacy issues		
Help and support in parenting issues		
Help with organization and priorities		
Help and support with social issues		
Feeling unable to resolve issues between you		
Needing change		
Issues regarding infidelity		
Trying to rebuild your relationship after a breakup/crisis		
Not wanting to repeat the same mistakes as in past relationships		
Help and support while considering future marriage		
Reassurance and validation for feelings/difficulties		
Help to control anger/meltdowns		
Looking to end the relationship		

When you have both completed the list, share with each other. Look for the ones you share and discuss the ones you don't. Take your agenda lists along with you to your first session, so you can give a copy to your therapist.

Arranging your first session

When you arrange your first session, try to do it by phone rather than email or text. This will give you the chance to talk to the therapist in person. This may be particularly important for the AS partner as it will give them the opportunity to decide if they like the sound of the therapist's voice. It is quite rare, but I have worked with an AS client who was sensitive to how another spoke and for all the best intentions in the world could not tolerate specific voice tones or accents for long. If this is the case, it would be best to make sure first that the AS partner is comfortable with the therapist's voice pitch or accent, rather than wasting both money and time.

When you call to talk to the therapist, ask them about their experience of both couple therapy and autism. How long have they worked in this area? How many clients on the spectrum have they seen? How long have they been working with couples? What workshops have they attended on working with AS/NT couples? Work experience is important, but equally important is personal experience of autism. I have found that the best therapists in this area will have had personal experience of autism, often with a partner, family or close friend. Having personal experience can make a difference, although it is important that the experience has not left the therapist biased or opinionated. It is very important that you see someone who knows and understands the issues you both face, but equally that they are not biased by their experience of autism. One couple I worked with discussed a therapist they had previously seen, who had advertised her expertise based on her own personal experience of living with autism. In their sessions, the therapist focused only on the negative aspects of autism and made the AS client feel worthless and dysfunctional and the NT partner feel stripped of all the hope they had of putting the marriage back on track. It took a long time for this couple to rebuild the relationship, and I fear the damage caused by the therapist will remain with them both.

Preparing for your first session

The first session will be an assessment of what a couple are hoping to achieve and what the therapist feels they can offer. In addition, this will possibly include form filling, details of the financial commitment as well as the length of time available. Be sure that the therapy is within your financial budget, especially if it turns out to be long term. Be sure it is affordable to you both. Equally ensure that you both have the time available for what could be a long-term commitment. This might also involve considering childcare and, if one or both of you work shifts or your job requires you to be on call or travel away, how you will fit the sessions in.

If you feel you would benefit from longer sessions or fortnightly rather than weekly sessions, discuss this with your prospective therapist. Remember that these sessions are for you, based on your needs and agenda. Providing that your requests are reasonable, if the therapist cannot work with your agenda, then maybe you should look elsewhere.

Take your couple therapy agendas with you for the first session and share them with the therapist to check it is something they feel able to work with.

After the session, discuss as a couple whether you both feel comfortable working with the therapist. It is important that the therapist feels right for both of you and is someone you feel you can trust.

Trust is very important in therapy; after all, you are offering the therapist the care of the most precious thing you share with your partner – your relationship. You both need to believe and trust that the therapist will look after your relationship and treat it with the respect it deserves.

Couple therapy versus individual therapy

If you and your partner decide to go for couple therapy, then it should be just that, couple therapy. I find that often couples go for therapy together only to find themselves being advised by the therapist to attend the sessions with them separately. It is in my experience, based on information I have received from couples, that this is rarely successful and can drive an even deeper wedge between the couple than they came with.

Many AS/NT couples seek therapy because they are struggling to connect together, cannot communicate and can find no common ground to work from and build their relationship together. Therapy should be about helping to educate and support the couple to come together and develop a better understanding of each other's perspective and world. This cannot be achieved if they are both seeing the therapist separately. The only person in this scenario who will benefit will be the therapist as it may be easier for them to see these two very different people separately. Unless both partners in the relationship request individual therapy, they should be seen together.

However, if the therapist feels that one partner is dealing with issues related to their childhood or a previous abusive relationship prior to meeting their partner or a traumatic event that is not related to their present relationship, then the partner should possibly be referred for individual therapy elsewhere to resolve these issues first, and then resume couple therapy together afterwards.

The only other time it is recommended for a couple to be seen separately is in the advent of, or threat of, domestic abuse, and this is a completely different issue from the main subject of this book. Having AS or living with someone on the spectrum is never a cause or reason for physical abuse. If either partner is violent or abusive, that is down to who they are and not whether they have or live with someone on the spectrum.

When therapy ends

There is no exact time span that can be recommended for length of therapy. What is important is that positive change is occurring in the relationship and both partners feel the benefit; if this is the case then therapy should continue. This might not occur straight away, but after six sessions it is expected that some change will have occurred. This will be assessed and discussed in the reviews you share with your therapist.

The therapist should have informed you at the start how often these reviews will take place – normally every four sessions, sometimes six.

Ending at the right time is very important in therapy and must feel right for everyone. Sometimes ending the sessions will feel just natural as a couple finds they are bringing less and less to the sessions. The therapist will be aware of this and may suggest that the time is coming to end the sessions.

For the couples I have seen I offer the option of coming back for what we call an MOT session. It may be that three or six months or even a year after our sessions end tensions start to build up again or the couple encounter an issue or problem they cannot resolve. The couple can return, and we work specifically on that agenda; often this only requires one or two sessions. Ask your therapist if they are happy to offer this as an option.

There is no guarantee that therapy will work for you. This is dependent on a number of variables, but the main ones are whether there is enough love, respect, trust and commitment left in the relationship and whether the therapist can empathize and understand the dynamics of an AS/NT relationship. Successful therapy will also partly depend on whether the partner with AS has been diagnosed and accepts that they are on the spectrum.

Chapter 13

TO HAVE OR NOT HAVE A DIAGNOSIS

FINDING somewhere to go for a diagnosis is, in my opinion, for most couples an absolute nightmare! The resources are so limited and underfunded. I receive many emails from individuals all over the world struggling to find somewhere they can go and to find someone they can see who is within their financial budget.

Having a diagnosis can make the difference between a couple staying together or not. Whether to seek a diagnosis is a major decision for an individual, and it is important that time and consideration are given to making this decision and that you explore together your reasons and motives.

As I did for the decision to go for therapy, I will discuss in this chapter some of the important points you should consider when deciding to seek a diagnosis. I hope this will raise some valid discussion points for any individual considering this route, and their partner.

How do I find someone to see for a diagnosis?

The first port of call for most is their general practitioner (GP) to ask their opinion and for a referral. Unfortunately, the outcome will depend very much on the GP's understanding of autism at the higher functioning or milder end of the spectrum. It has become apparent from some of my clients that their GP only understood the more severe aspects of autism, with clients being told on the basis of their employment, education and relationship, or the fact that they could make the phone call, that they could not be on the autistic spectrum.

Not all GPs fully understand the knock-on effect this can have on an individual or their relationship. When someone has reached a point in their lives of accepting that they might be on the spectrum and has the desire to find out why they are struggling at work or in relationships, why they are finding some things so difficult that do not even seem to concern others and why they are so affected by their senses, it can be cruel and disheartening to be turned away as though they should be grateful for being disregarded. They have finally been brave enough and had the confidence to approach what should be a knowledgeable expert, and they reach a brick wall.

All individuals on the spectrum are different and will present very differently. Many AS adults, particularly women, will have learned well how to put on the mask and disguise the anxiety, the confusion and low self-esteem that they are suffering. A five-minute consultation will not give any GP, psychologist, psychiatrist or specialist enough time to decide whether someone is or isn't affected by an ASC.

If anyone is unfortunate enough to find themselves in this situation then you have every right to disagree and ask to be referred to someone who does understand what being on the higher functioning end of the spectrum means.

Choosing to have a private diagnosis

For some individuals, the idea of having an autistic spectrum condition stamped on their medical records is not a comfortable one, as there is the fear that they will have to disclose this when they apply for employment and insurance or contact various agencies. There is the fear it could prevent the individual from finding, and keeping, employment or cause them to be penalized because of the diagnosis. Although this could certainly have been the case 20 years ago, much has changed now, and an individual has the right to challenge decisions made by organizations if they are felt to be biased. Much of the stigma has been removed, but unfortunately, often due to lack of education and simple ignorance, bias does still exist and there have been reports of individuals feeling they are penalized for being on the spectrum.

The pros and cons of seeking a private diagnosis

The pros:

- Puts control in the individual's hands.

- Allows a choice of clinicians or specialists.

- Allows negotiation for a date and time for the assessment.

- Is completely confidential to you alone.

- Does not have to be put on medical records.

- It is entirely up to the individual who they tell.

The cons:

- Can be very expensive.

- The assessment may not be accepted by all authorities, especially if it is for a court case, custody battle, benefits or insurance claim. A formal clinical diagnosis may be needed for legal cases.

I was very surprised when I recently did a search to find how much was being charged for a diagnosis. In some cases, it came to thousands of pounds. I feel individuals on the spectrum are being exploited due to the limited resources on offer.

It is entirely up to the individual and couple as to which route they take and how much they can afford. The important point is that the person seeking the diagnosis is doing it for the right reasons.

Who is the diagnosis for?

When working with a client who expresses that they wish to be assessed for an autistic spectrum condition, I enquire as to why they want to know if they have an ASC. I find that clients can often be divided into two separate groups.

The 'just wanting confirmation' group are the individuals who, due to their own research or the possibility being suggested by their partner or a friend, have reached a point where they just want to find out if one or both of them are on the spectrum. I see more and more women on the spectrum who have arrived at this place in their life's journey and want answers regarding whether there is a reason for their struggles and feeling different.

Many in this group have already self-diagnosed and are simply seeking validation. It is unusual for them to be wrong as they know themselves better than anyone, including the clinician performing the assessment. So, it comes as no surprise to them when their suppositions are confirmed.

Then there is the 'coerced' group. This is the group that both pays and comes along for an assessment when they really don't want to be there. These people are the most difficult to accurately diagnose, because diagnosis depends on the honesty of the person and is largely dependent on the answers given to the questions that the clinician asks. It does not take a lot of research for anyone to work out what answers should be given to avoid a positive diagnosis. Autism at this high-functioning level is not always obvious and, unlike a physical ailment, there is no physical test that can be delivered and it is highly dependent on the self-reporting and answers given.

The most common reason these individuals seek a diagnosis is to prove to their partner that they are not on the spectrum and it is only because of their partner that they agreed to be assessed. The reason this happens is that it is often the NT partner who is the first to recognize the possibility of autism. Many times, this is due to a child being positively diagnosed as on the spectrum or it may be through something they read or the suggestion of a friend. The NT partner may do their own research and take time to accumulate all the facts they can before they approach their partner with this new revelation. It is a way for the NT partner to try to make sense of the things their partner states, their sometimes confusing behaviour and why there are so many unresolved issues in the relationship. It can come as a great relief to many NT partners to believe they have found a reason for the way things have been. Sometimes this information is taken well by the AS partner, who will soon be researching and finding out for themselves whether this information is accurate and applies to them.

Sometimes, though, this information is not received well by the AS partner and is taken as an extreme form of criticism from the NT partner. Total denial takes place and arguments ensue, which can be stressful and upsetting for both. Ultimatums are given, and the partner presumed to be on the spectrum will do anything to prove they are not, including going for an assessment. Often when asking a client why they want to be assessed I have been given the answer, 'Because I want to prove to my partner I haven't got it!' In most cases, they will do just that, even if the clinician strongly suspects otherwise. If they do not tick the boxes to fulfil the diagnostic criteria, they cannot be given a positive diagnosis as their answers have to be accepted and believed to be accurate and true. This is the saddest scenario of all and for most couples will mark the start of the end of their relationship as neither will trust the other again.

How long will a diagnosis take?

This varies greatly. If the assessment is simply to determine whether the individual is affected by autism and not complicated by other conditions, then an assessment should take approximately three to four hours. Certainly, a decision should be reached within one day.

I have heard of individuals being diagnosed within as little as ten minutes and in most of these cases being told they were not on the spectrum. It is impossible to make an accurate diagnosis in such a short time. However, some clinicians can require several sessions spread out over a few weeks. There do not seem to be any definite rules about this.

Do I have to go alone, or do I have to take someone with me?

I would recommend, if possible, that a partner (or, if applicable, a parent) attends the assessment too. Although it is the answers given by the individual being assessed that will count the most, it is useful for the clinician to hear from another perspective, especially if they can help with the history taking. Many NT partners discover much about their partner that they were not aware of in the past, especially about their childhood and adolescence. Listening to the specific questions the clinician asks and the areas they explore will help the NT partner to become more aware of the characteristics of autism that relate to their partner. It also can be useful for the NT partner to take notes and act as a memory aid after the assessment, as information can be easily lost if the AS person is feeling stressed.

Just as with couple therapy, going together for an assessment should be a shared experience for a couple and an experience that will bring them closer together. Being in a mixed relationship will affect both partners, not just one, and it is important that the two partners share this journey together and understand what it means for both.

When will I get the results?

It is far better if results are given on the same day as attending the assessment. I believe that this is very important and particularly in the case of assessing for autism as individuals on the spectrum can become very anxious if kept waiting for too long.

A good and experienced clinician will know at the end of the assessment whether the diagnosis is positive or negative, so why is that information often withheld?

Some clinicians will wish to seek the advice of another, often a more experienced, clinician first. They will take their notes and thoughts to another to see if they agree or disagree with their results. This is understandable if the case is complicated or there is the suspicion that the symptoms are not related to autism but are the result of another condition. Equally, it will delay the results if there is the concern that there is a case of co-morbidity, meaning that more than one condition is occurring. If the clinician suspects this then the client should be informed that this is something they need further advice on, or further testing.

Another reason the information may not be given at the end of the assessment is because the clinician would rather give this information by letter or in some cases by email. This is not the best way to deliver information as sensitive as this and does not allow the client the opportunity to ask any relevant questions they have or queries about the results.

Find out before you arrange an assessment exactly how and when you will be given the results. In addition, establish what support you can expect after the assessment.

What if I do not agree with the results?

If after the assessment you are given a negative or positive diagnosis and this is not what you expected, you have the right to challenge this and ask why the decision has been reached. If you are still not satisfied, you have the option to seek a second opinion, although this will bring with it more costs.

What can I expect after a positive assessment?

There can be a slight anti-climax after an assessment. At the end of the assessment the AS partner might feel drained, tired and totally exhausted from all the questions, self-analysing and history taking they have experienced. It may be that the validation comes as quite a shock and not what the individual or their partner expected, and this can produce quite a cocktail of negative emotions. Time will be needed to process the information, and it is important that the couple take that time, sometimes together, sometimes alone, to do this. If the negative feelings persist then it could help to seek advice and support from a professional. Sometimes these negative feelings are caused by a lack of understanding as to what being on the spectrum means. It could be that there is confusion as to what aspects of the individual are due to being on the spectrum and what is down to personality; what is the scope for change? For a couple, it can raise many questions about what it means for their relationship, such as:

- What can we do to improve our relationship?

- What can be changed and improved?

- What cannot change?

- Can we still have a relationship?

The post-diagnosis period can feel confusing and overwhelming. Professional support is sometimes needed at this time, and working with a therapist who offers patience, support and education can be of great benefit and help both partners feel more in control regarding how they go forward.

Assessment and diagnosis can also be a positive experience for some clients and their partners. The AS partner might quite enjoy the experience of being allowed time to talk about themselves and their interests. From my experience, most of my clients have felt a tremendous sense of relief and, to their partner's surprise, have cried with joy. These overwhelming feelings of relief are because for so many clients it is the first time they have felt understood and been given a reason for why they have struggled. They now have a name for the way they have felt, the difficulties experienced in social situations, emotional communication and relationships. Suddenly, their childhood and their lives start to make sense and they are not responsible for the times they didn't get it right; it was because they didn't know they were getting it wrong. The relief is therapeutic and freeing. It can take days for this process to settle, so support and understanding from their partner will be more than beneficial right now.

Meanwhile, the NT partner will also be experiencing a tremendous medley of thoughts and feelings that could consist of relief, shock, guilt, love, hate, anger and loss. Loss can be the most dominant of these feelings because until the point of diagnosis there would have been hope of sharing a typical NT/NT relationship with their partner. That hope is now gone, and the reality of autism becomes unavoidable, even in their imagination and fantasies. I write much about this effect in my book written for NT partners, *The Other Half of Asperger Syndrome* (2014). Loss is a process that has to be experienced and in times like this can be quite unavoidable.

Ignorance is not bliss!

Life will not be the same after a positive diagnosis. The hope is that it will be better, because ignorance is not bliss and knowing the reasons why sometimes the relationship and communication are hard work really helps. Knowing means a couple can get appropriate support, read the right books and begin to develop and better their understanding of each other. Knowing means that a line can be drawn on the past, and an explanation for unresolved issues can now be given. Knowing means that changes can be made to help the relationship work better for both. Knowing means that the NT partner will be more aware of looking after their own needs and will seek emotional support from family, friends and other groups. Most importantly, they can now change the unrealistic expectations they had of their partner and replace them with something that is achievable. There are so many benefits to knowing, and if the couple have the love, commitment and incentive to work at their relationship, then things can only get better for both.

Unfortunately, this will not be the case for everyone, as sometimes by the time a diagnosis is sought it is too late for the relationship and one or both in the relationship are already too tired and exhausted to try anymore and consequently the couple decide to separate. If this is the case, then it is hoped that knowing will allow the couple to separate more amicably and in time go forward. Both now know what caused some of the problems and understand why things became so difficult.

Remember, it is a positive to know that it is autism that has been causing these breakdowns or misunderstandings and that neither partner is to blame. Understanding this can make a big difference to the couple, family and friends, but this raises the issue of who else to tell about the diagnosis.

• Chapter 14 •

WHO TO TELL ABOUT AUTISM

AFTER a diagnosis of autism, the couple may ask or wish to discuss who they should tell about the diagnosis. Sometimes there may be a difference of opinion between the couple. The AS partner may not want anyone to know for fear that it will be used against them, or that it suggests they are inferior in some way. Others may not care who knows and see it as irrelevant. One client once said to me, 'What does it matter? I am still me!'

The NT partner would often like to tell everyone, for at last they know they are not going mad and it was not solely their fault that things were breaking down – it was because of autism. Careful consideration needs to be given to this. It is important to respect the wishes of the AS partner, as long as they are being reasonable and considering all involved. My message to clients is to tell only those where some benefit to the couple is to be gained. It is very important that no one suffers as a consequence of knowing, especially the person with the diagnosis.

The first people the couple often think of to tell are their children. Obviously, this is very dependent on how old the children are and what the circumstances are. It is, however, a point worth discussing in this book. Children of parents affected by autism can often feel they have not been emotionally supported by the AS parent. They will be aware that the parent may have worked to provide them with the material things they need, but they are unlikely to have felt emotionally valued. Equally, the children can often feel they are valued for what they do rather than for who they are. Again, due to the difficulty in applying theory of mind, the AS parent is sometimes unable to see things from their children's perspective. The AS parent may often not be aware that there is something they are not doing for their children. If the children do not know or understand why, they are likely to take it personally and may feel emotionally neglected by the parent, believing it to be intentional.

Understanding why their AS parent behaves the way they do can make a huge difference. Knowing can allow the child to learn how best to communicate with their AS parent and how to recognize the signs that the parent does care very much for them, although this is often expressed in what the parent does rather than any verbal or physical expressions of love.

For example, one AS parent described how much time they gave to transporting their child to and from private music lessons or dance classes. When their child accused them of never being there for them, they were shocked and deeply hurt by this, feeling that all this effort was not valued.

When the child understood autism and how their parent struggled with emotional expression and had difficulty, unless informed, understanding what was going on in another's world, they could learn that it was not personal or because their AS parent was not interested in their thoughts. To have this reinforced by a third party such as a therapist can result in the parent's situation being taken more seriously by the child and allows the child the opportunity to freely express how it makes them feel and explore any questions they might want to ask without fear of hurting anyone's feelings.

Sometimes parents struggle with how to tell children about autism, especially if they are quite young. I suggest it would not be helpful to try to explain autism to a child below the age of six. I have devised a way of explaining autism that I find can work well as it gives a realistic and practical demonstration of how the AS parent is affected.

A practical way to demonstrate communication difficulties to a child

- Ask the child to put on a blindfold or to cover their eyes so they cannot see.
- Give them a big smile.
- Now ask them to tell you what you are doing with your face.
- When the child says they cannot see you to say what you are doing, tell them you were giving a big smile.
- Ask them why they did not smile back.
- Repeat points 2 to 5, but this time stick your tongue out at them.
- When the child says again they do not know what you are doing, tell them you're sticking your tongue out at them because they did not smile back.
- Take off the blindfold.
- Explain to the child that this is what it is like for Mummy/Daddy, saying they cannot tell what you are thinking or how you are feeling unless you tell them clearly in words.
- Explain this is how things get misunderstood sometimes because Mummy/Daddy has not understood that they were trying to be friendly and misunderstood their intentions, so responded negatively.
- If you have a recent example you can tell the child about, then use it now.

A practical way to explain the effect of social interaction to a child

- Ask the child to put the blindfold back on.
- Ask them to have a go at walking across the room (make sure there is nothing dangerous in the way and you are by their side).
- When they begin to try this, ask them if they would like you to tell them if there is something in front of them.
- Give them directions in order that they can walk across a room.
- Take off the blindfold.
- Explain that this is what it is like when Mummy/Daddy come into a room, especially if there is lots going on.
- Explain how it is really hard for them to know what is going on, just like it was hard for the child to know what was in their way.
- Understanding that Mummy/Daddy has this difficulty will mean they can help by explaining what is happening, in the same way the directions helped them across the room.
- Explain that when you cannot see it will take longer to move around, just like it takes Mummy/Daddy longer to understand what is happening or what you want them to do, if you do not tell them.
- Explain how if someone could not see, you would not put something in their way that they would not expect, like moving the furniture around and not telling them about it. This can be used to explain how something unpredictable or unexpected can be very difficult for Mummy/Daddy.
- Explain to the child that this is what it can be like to have autism.

Keep this whole exercise fun while maintaining the importance of it for both the child and the AS parent to understand one another. It is important that as well as understanding the areas that the AS parent may find difficult, the child understands the talents and skills the AS parent has and the contribution they make to the family.

Telling parents

The next people to discuss telling are often the parents and in-laws of the AS partner. The first thing to consider is the age of the parents concerned. If we are talking about a very elderly person, then you need to ask what benefit there will be in telling them. Often there will be none. The next question to ask is whether they need to know. Making a pros and cons list of benefits against disadvantages might help before disclosure.

Bear in mind that since autism is genetic, one or other of the AS partner's parents may be on the spectrum too, which could potentially lead to a total denial of the diagnosis. This denial can be for two reasons: it is possible that because the person is also on the spectrum they do not see their child's behaviour as different from their own; it is also possible that they do not want to contemplate the fact their offspring is affected by what is, to all intents and purposes, seen as a disability.

Sometimes the result of disclosure can be extreme, and the NT partner is blamed, finding themselves then excluded from the family and not spoken to again, leaving the AS partner in a very difficult position. If there's a likelihood of such an extreme reaction, there is no benefit in disclosure.

Telling friends

Once again, ask the questions: What are the benefits? Do they need to know? More often than not it is the NT partner, especially if they are female, who wants to tell their friends. The NT partner will have experienced a level of emotional deprivation and will probably have discussed their situation with close friends, so the diagnosis can be a watershed insofar as they can now rationalize to their friends the situation they have been in. For example, female NT partners often hear from friends, 'He's just behaving like a man', or may be asked by friends, 'Why are you complaining? He really cares about you.' To be able to say 'This is not male behaviour, it is autism' or 'Yes, he does care, but there are some things he is not able to give me' can help validate her existence and restore some of her self-esteem.

Think about the possibility that friends or partners of friends may be on the spectrum too. Consider how and who the AS partner relates to among friends. People affected by autism socialize very well with people who perhaps share their 'special interest'. Sometimes, friends of the NT partner discover that their own partners also have autism, so the disclosure has actually helped them. Once again, it is something the couple need to decide together.

Employers and colleagues at work

Deciding to tell one's employer or, for that matter, one's work colleagues can be risky ground for the AS partner. Try asking a few people if they know what autism is and I think you'll realize how little is still known about it. One client I worked with told his employers and found this worked against him. Their perspective of him changed and, due to his employers' lack of understanding, found he was questioned about his capabilities to fulfil certain tasks, thus undermining his confidence and ultimately leading to losing his job. There was definitely zero benefit there.

I have worked not only with AS clients who have difficulties in employment but also with some of their employers to very good effect, and some more forward-thinking agencies highly value the many qualities that being on the spectrum can bring.

On the following page I have put together a list of the possible benefits and pitfalls of telling others, which I hope will allow the couple to discuss and decide who to tell.

WORKSHEET

Example of a Post-Diagnosis Who to Tell List

Person to tell	Benefits	Costs
Dad	Help him to understand himself	He may feel responsible
Mum	Help her to understand both her husband and son	She may feel let down that no one pointed this out to her before (especially professionals)
Dan and Emily	Explain why Dad behaves as he does sometimes	They may worry that they or their future children may be on the spectrum
Lily	Too young	Too young to understand
Boss	Possibly result in making some changes at work	Could result in discrimination
Best friend	Help him/her to understand why I get it wrong sometimes	Might change his/her perspective of me for the worse

▬ Instructions for the Post-Diagnosis Who to Tell List

1. Both have a Who to Tell List.

2. Both decide together on all the relevant people who might be told about autism.

3. Enter the person's name on each list.

4. Fill in the Benefits and Costs columns separately.

5. Compare together what each of you have written down.

6. Decide together who would gain from being told.

WORKSHEET

Post-Diagnosis Who to Tell List

Person to tell	Benefits	Costs

The terminology or wording when telling someone about a diagnosis is important. For example, rather than saying 'I have autism', which suggests that you've caught something, say 'I am affected by autism', which is like saying 'Strong light affects my eyes.' The latter tends to retain who the person is and does not personally label them. I emphasize in my work that autism only affects a small part of the brain; it does not change a person's personality. Their hopes, their dreams, their desires are no different from the rest of the population. If a person has the potential to be good at something, they may be even better at it because of being affected by autism. If there was something they were potentially not good at, then likewise they will be less good at it as they will not see the point in trying hard at something they do not enjoy.

Just as it is important to recognize that autism will not take away a person's identity or change who they are, it is equally important to recognize that living with a partner with autism may affect the self-identity of the non-AS partner. This effect is called Cassandra.

• Chapter 15 •

WHAT IS CASSANDRA?

CASSANDRA is becoming a recognized and common term that refers to the NT partner, whether male or female, if they feel that the relationship has had a negative effect on their self-esteem, confidence or mental health. The term Cassandra comes from Greek mythology. Cassandra was a mortal who became the focus of the god Apollo's romantic intentions. In an effort to win the love of the beautiful Cassandra, he gave her the gift of foresight. However, when Cassandra rejected Apollo's romantic intentions, he cursed her by making it so that no one would ever believe the things she told them. This feeling of not being believed is typical of how many NT people feel when living with a person with undiagnosed autism.

Over the years, the terminology for the effect of Cassandra has changed. Before the term Cassandra, it was referred to as the mirror syndrome by the Families of Adults Affected by Asperger's Syndrome (FAAAS) and then referred to as the Cassandra phenomenon (Rodman 2003). The Cassandra phenomenon was first made public at an FAAAS conference in 2003 and termed as Cassandra affective disorder (CAD) (Aston 2003a). Finally, the term affective deprivation disorder (AfDD) was used as it is a condition that is not purely exclusive to AS/NT relationships and is caused by living with a partner who has a low emotional intelligence, which is often the result of alexithymia, a sub-category condition that affects over 50 per cent of individuals on the spectrum. In this chapter, I will refer to this transitional relational condition as the Cassandra phenomenon or Cassandra, as that is now the most common term used.

The Cassandra phenomenon (CP) does not discriminate and can affect the NT person at any age, whether they are male or female and regardless of whether the relationship is heterosexual, homosexual or lesbian. CP is a secondary condition and based on a person's situation. It is transitional as it is a consequence of long-term stress that can build up in the relationship and is not a personality disorder. Emotional reciprocity, love and belonging are essential human needs. If these needs are not being met and the reason why is not understood, mental and physical health due to long-term stress may be affected.

CP is the result of emotional deprivation due to the fact that the AS partner is not always able to provide the emotional support the NT partner needs to stay healthy within the relationship. This is further enhanced if the AS partner is also affected by alexithymia. An important point that needs to be made clear is that this effect on the NT partner is rarely intentional on the part of the AS partner, who is often shocked and saddened when they realize how the relationship is affecting their loved one/s. Unfortunately, the negative feelings the NT is experiencing are often exacerbated by the lack of support and understanding offered to them by family, friends and sadly professionals too.

Often when the NT partner tries to explain how they feel to a friend or therapist, they find themselves apologizing for how trivial they sound and some question whether they are excessive complainers. One NT partner once said to me, 'You must think I am harping on about nothing. I am not one to complain but I feel that it is all I do now because nothing ever changes. There is no learning, and no one seems to understand what I am talking about.' This is typical of how it can feel for the NT partner, who will have a history of not being believed when they know all too well that what they are describing is true. This is especially the case when the NT partner is not aware that their relationship is affected by autism and is struggling to work out what it is that isn't working and why, no matter how hard they try, they cannot put it right.

This time is the most difficult for the NT partner as they come to realize that all the strategies and skills they employed in past relationships just aren't working in this relationship. It is a time when they start to search for answers and can, if the answers aren't forthcoming, find themselves becoming over-obsessed with everything their partner does or says, looking for clues.

Some NT partners try desperately to find something they can blame the misunderstanding on; this might be their partner's childhood, if they feel his parents were not very affectionate or remote and distant. It might be that their partner was sent to a boarding school or maybe they were bullied at school. The problems could be blamed on a previous negative relationship experience that their partner endured or, if no feasible reason is found, some NT partners will start to blame themselves.

If this continues then the NT partner will find that the relationship begins to take over all their thoughts, feelings and conversations; friends might become frustrated as they feel they are hearing the same set of reoccurring issues being discussed, with no change. The NT partner might begin to distance themselves from friends and hobbies as they have no energy left to enjoy them since their relationship is all they can endure.

Meanwhile, the AS partner will be aware that their partner is unhappy, but they will not know why or what they are expected to do about it. They might have found that, when they did try, they got it wrong and felt rebuffed or that they failed.

Consequently, they will not try again and will distance themselves even more from their partner. This will exacerbate their partner's feelings of aloneness and enhance their growing obsession with trying to find a reason for the issues that keep occurring.

I liken this to the term 'Groundhog Day' as it can feel for the NT partner that the pattern keeps repeating itself again and again and again. This can cause the issues to became all-consuming and seem hopelessly unsolvable.

Even if eventually the reason for the difficulties are discovered and the NT partner is aware now that their partner is affected by autism and as such not deliberately causing the emotional deprivation, this will not automatically prevent the CP if it has been going on for a long time. Sometimes this knowledge can make it harder for the NT partner, especially if they believe that now they both know the reason, everything will automatically be fixed. It will take time and effort to break this cycle and together work out a way forward which is healthy for both of them.

Expectations will have to change, and a more realistic and workable relationship will need to be put into place. Both will have to work at this without feeling guilty or attaching blame. The AS partner cannot spontaneously offer the emotional reciprocity their partner needs without some form of instruction or explanation. This is something that for the AS partner is not within their capacity, any more than a visually impaired adult can suddenly acquire crystal-clear vision without a pair of spectacles. This is why I emphasize a stratagem of no blame.

What causes the Cassandra phenomenon?

The easiest way to understand CP is to relate it to seasonal affective disorder (SAD). SAD is caused by sunlight deprivation, which can create a neurochemical imbalance in the brain. This can result in sleep problems, lethargy, overeating, depression, loss of self-esteem, hopelessness, social problems and a desire to avoid social contact, anxiety, tension, a loss of libido, mood changes and signs of a weakened immune system. SAD is very real. However, where SAD is about sunlight deprivation, CP is about emotional deprivation. The CP sufferer experiences similar symptoms to those of the SAD sufferer. But there is a more damaging effect on the CP sufferer insofar as it is not seasonal but due to their full-time relationship. Although finding out about autism provides an explanation as to what is happening in the relationship, this knowledge alone cannot fix it. The NT partner will have to come to terms with the fact that this is not going to change. Accepting that the AS partner is not to blame and that they are not intentionally depriving them of the emotional support they need will take time and hard work. In addition, some NT partners recognize they have a parent who is on the spectrum too, and once again must come to terms with the effect this has had with their relationship with this parent.

The fact that it is unintentional is only realized when the reason for the behaviour is discovered either by self-diagnosis or preferably diagnosis by a professional. Living in a relationship where autism is undiagnosed or denied will often result in the NT person being blamed for the problems in the relationship by their partner, family, friends and society. In society, it is often the very people who should be supporting the NT partners and their families who let them down – doctors, counsellors, therapists, teachers and psychologists – all through a lack of awareness of autism and its effects. They choose not to believe the NT person and view them as the one with the problem. The effects of CP are likely to be at their height when the NT person (male or female) finds themselves in the position of not being believed by the AS partner, parent, friends, family and professionals.

These feelings of confusion, aloneness, desperation and not being believed have resulted in the name Cassandra being applied to the condition.

What are the symptoms of CP?
Emotional health

- Low self-esteem

- Feeling confused/bewildered

- Feelings of anger

- Feelings of guilt

- Loss of self-identity.

Mental health

- Anger turns to depression

- Anxiety

- Phobias/social agoraphobia

- Adopting autistic traits

- Self-neglect.

Physical health

- Migraines

- Loss or gain in weight

- Premenstrual tension/female-related problems

- Low immune system.

What can be done to prevent CP?

Awareness and understanding are paramount in eliminating the condition. As CP is a consequence of the person's situation, it is therefore possible to find ways to alter that situation. Relationships where one partner has AS can succeed if both partners understand their differences and work on developing a better or different way of communicating. I advise that this is undertaken with a therapist who understands CP. If that is not possible, then the couple or family can use the strategies offered in this book and work together to improve the relationship.

The effects of CP can be reduced if both partners accept and understand why it occurs in the first place. This is unlikely to happen if there has been no diagnosis or acceptance that autism exists in a partner. Realization that the problems in the relationship are the consequence of the neurological differences between their respective emotional and psychological needs can be the first step to recovery. Diagnosis by a professional of the partner's autism or even self-diagnosis can offer answers to many questions and unexplained events and situations that have occurred in the relationship. It offers a reason for the breakdowns in communication, the embarrassing moments or avoidance of social situations. Most of all, it tells both partners that neither is going mad and neither is to blame for the difficulties they have experienced.

The acceptance of autism can be the beginning of a new type of relationship. By developing understanding of the different way each processes information, good communication can begin. Using strategies such as those supplied in this workbook, reading the experiences of other couples affected by autism, looking at the research available and finding a therapist who is able to offer understanding to both partners will help the couple develop a better understanding of each other.

CP is about a lack of spontaneous emotional reciprocity which should be seen as a type of food that is crucial to the emotional survival of the NT partner and which, if not received, will see self-esteem, self-confidence and self-identity damaged. The NT partner will need to spend time with like-minded people (other zebras!) doing the things that they enjoy. This does not mean there is nothing the AS partner can do. If their partner is feeling emotionally fed and content, then all will benefit. On the following page I have provided a list for both partners to consider and discuss together as to what is applicable to them and what might be practicably put into action.

▬ Instructions for Preventing Cassandra worksheets

1. Find some time when you can discuss these together and not be disturbed.

2. Both look at your appropriate list and tick the ones that you would like to do or are already doing.

3. Discuss these together as to how you might fit them in.

4. Use the blank sheets to fill in your own list.

5. Put them up on the wall in a prominent position so they will be noticed every day.

WORKSHEET
Preventing Cassandra – for the NT partner

	TICK
Meet up with friend/s	
Join a gym	
Take up a creative pastime	
Join a ramblers/running club	
Join an internet support group	
Learn to pamper yourself, e.g. hairdresser/pedicure/massage	
Have a coffee morning	
Make use of your spiritual/religious group for support	
Spoil yourself with something nice	
Keep a feelings journal/diary	

WORKSHEET

Preventing Cassandra – for the AS partner

	TICK
Give your partner a kiss when you are leaving the house	
Greet your partner when you get home	
Greet your partner when they arrive home	
Say one nice thing to your partner every day	
If your partner is upset, ask if they would like a hug	
Give your partner a hug before you go to sleep	
Hold your partner's hand when you are walking together	
Ask your partner what sort of day they have had	
Remember to call home if you are going to be late	
Tell your partner you love them, even if you have said it before	
Send your partner a nice text message	
Leave a post-it note for your partner to find with a nice message	

Preventing Cassandra – for the NT partner

	TICK

WORKSHEET

Preventing Cassandra – for the AS partner

	TICK

Once again it is about trial and error, but if the incentive, motivation and commitment of the couple to make their relationship work are there, then by accepting and understanding the differences, difference can work. It will be hard work. There are no miracle cures. It is about focusing on the positives and working through the negatives. It will invariably be the NT partner who will feel they are putting in the most effort, as it is the NT partner who is more able to be flexible and make changes. The NT partner will be learning to manage in an autistic world. They will only be able to do this if they accept that there are some things their AS partner will not be able to provide which they will have to look for elsewhere or through other means.

For some couples, whatever they do, the relationship will not work and therefore the decision has to be made as to whether they stay in the relationship or not. Harsh as this may sound, it is sometimes the reality. However, I do say to the NT partner that if they are planning to end the relationship, do so because of who their partner is and not because of autism. Autism affects all personality types. If two personalities are not compatible, they will still be incompatible whether one partner has autism or not.

Autism brings positives and negatives to a relationship. Some couples are able to work with the negatives, accepting the difference and continuing to love one another. If the AS partner is in denial of their condition, they will more than likely blame their NT partner for all the problems in the relationship. If this is the case, then decisions need to be made as to how the relationship goes forward. Again, seeking out an appropriate therapist may be worthwhile for the couple to decide whether the relationship is at an end.

If a relationship does end, it is more likely to be due to personality clash and incompatibility than whether someone is affected by autism. I have worked with over two thousand couples and I have found that the majority of relationships do work and the couples love each other very much. However, relationships need to be maintained and nurtured regardless of whether they are affected by autism, and this will require the effort and time of both partners.

Chapter 16

MAINTAINING THE RELATIONSHIP TOGETHER

MAINTAINING the relationship is essential if it is going to remain healthy and functioning. Maintenance takes time, effort and motivation, and is not always given the credit and relevance it deserves. In fact, our relationship is often one of the most neglected areas of our lives. Imagine if relationships were evaluated in the same way many people are evaluated in their job or business. How long would that employment or business survive if no one upheld their job role or put any effort into it? It wouldn't be long before someone found themselves out of a job, redundant or, the worse-case scenario, bankrupt!

The same applies to relationships. It is very easy that once a couple are living together or joined together in marriage or a civil partnership they take the other partner for granted and, rather than thinking about their partner's needs and desires, become totally self-absorbed in focusing on their own. This can cause a build-up of resentment, cynicism and blame, which will result in distancing, stonewalling and, at the worse, separation or divorce.

So how can a couple avoid this debacle from materializing in their relationship? What can be put in place to prevent it?

Planning ahead and setting aside a definite time to spend together and discuss issues can prevent aggravations and misunderstandings from building up. It is very easy to lose touch with what is going on in the other partner's world. This is especially true in the case of an AS/NT relationship when communication may not be as free flowing and forthcoming as it could be.

Life's daily stressors and aggravators can quickly build up and overwhelm us. It is easy to find ourselves becoming self-absorbed as we work our way through a conundrum of problems and issues that require our attention and steal our spare time. It won't take long before both in the relationship are feeling somewhat alone, neglected and completely out of touch with their partner and their partner's world.

To make changes requires the effort of both partners. First of all, a pre-planned time will need to be arranged for you both to sit down together undisturbed on a weekly basis, if possible. Second, each will need a written agenda of what they want to discuss. This could be forthcoming events and dates for the diary, it could be jobs and tasks that need doing around the house, with the car or garden. It could be time to take some pebbles out of the bucket to try to resolve any issues that are still causing disquiet.

These meetings will allow time to oversee and evaluate the relationship. The meetings could be compared to attending a job review and, like a job review, there will need to be some rules attached. I have listed these rules for meetings here:

- Pick a regular time that can (if possible) be fulfilled once a week.

- Ensure that neither of you will be disturbed.

- Do not take mobile phones into the meeting.

- Do not have the radio or television on in the background.

- Set a time limit – no more than one hour.

- Do not allow arguing. If an argument erupts then the meeting is to be closed and only resumed when both are calm.

- Make sure you have prioritized your agenda list and given a copy to your partner at least an hour before the meeting.

- Allow each partner a maximum of 15 minutes per item on their agenda list.

- After 15 minutes (or less if completed), allow the other partner to share their agenda.

- Ensure that each partner has an equal amount of time.

- Take notes if helpful.

- Anything unresolved or not discussed can be carried forward to the following week.

It is for each couple to arrange this together in a way that works for them. The two most important points are that it is fair and no one raises their voice or becomes abusive in any way.

Relationship assessment (RA) sheets

Another way to maintain the relationship is to monitor and assess how it is progressing. When working with couples I use my relationship assessment sheets that I put together for each couple. I base the statements on the difficulties or issues that have been highlighted in counselling. The couple's response to the statements is given in the way of numbers rather than words as this has a far better chance of success for the client on the spectrum and is still easily completed by the NT partner. Below is an example of a partly completed RA sheet.

Example of a partly completed Relationship Assessment Questionnaire

Relationship assessment: Please rate in numbers how much you agree with the statements below: 1 being the least and 10 being the most.

I trust my partner's fidelity

| 1 | 2 | 3 | 4 | 5 | 6 | 7 | 8 ✓ | 9 | 10 |

I trust my partner to make the right decisions

| 1 | 2 | 3 | 4 | 5 | 6 | 7 | 8 | 9 ✓ | 10 |

I trust my partner financially

| 1 | 2 | 3 | 4 | 5 | 6 | 7 | 8 | 9 ✓ | 10 |

I trust in my partner's care of our children

| 1 | 2 | 3 | 4 | 5 | 6 | 7 | 8 | 9 | 10 ✓ |

My partner makes me feel attractive

| 1 | 2 | 3 | 4 ✓ | 5 | 6 | 7 | 8 | 9 | 10 |

My partner makes me feel desirable

| 1 | 2 | 3 ✓ | 4 | 5 | 6 | 7 | 8 | 9 | 10 |

My partner makes me feel valuable

| 1 | 2 | 3 | 4 | 5 | 6 | 7 | 8 | 9 ✓ | 10 |

I find my partner attractive

| 1 | 2 | 3 | 4 | 5 | 6 | 7 | 8 | 9 ✓ | 10 |

I find my partner desirable

| 1 | 2 | 3 | 4 | 5 | 6 | 7 | 8 ✓ | 9 | 10 |

I am satisfied with our sex life

| 1 | 2 | 3 ✓ | 4 | 5 | 6 | 7 | 8 | 9 | 10 |

The example above shows very quickly that the problems occurring for this partner are in their sex life and how their partner makes them feel.

The sheets provided cover a whole array of areas that a couple might want to explore. If there are some statements that are not applicable, they can be crossed out; if there are any statements you would like to add, there are some empty spaces below. You will need to decide and agree on this together.

▬ Instructions for completing the Relationship Assessment Questionnaire

1. Find a time when you will not be disturbed and have time to concentrate and consider the statements contained.

2. Each partner is to have an identical sheet each.

3. Tick or put a circle round the number that best describes how strong you agree with the statement.

4. The higher the number, the stronger your agreement.

5. When completed, exchange sheets and compare them together. Discuss together at your next meeting or take with you to discuss with a therapist.

Relationship Assessment Questionnaire

Please rate in numbers how much you agree with the statements below: 1 being the least and 10 being the most.

I trust my partner's fidelity

1	2	3	4	5	6	7	8	9	10

I trust my partner to make the right decisions

1	2	3	4	5	6	7	8	9	10

I trust my partner financially

1	2	3	4	5	6	7	8	9	10

I trust in my partner's care of our children

1	2	3	4	5	6	7	8	9	10

My partner makes me feel attractive

1	2	3	4	5	6	7	8	9	10

My partner makes me feel desirable

1	2	3	4	5	6	7	8	9	10

My partner makes me feel valuable

1	2	3	4	5	6	7	8	9	10

I find my partner attractive

1	2	3	4	5	6	7	8	9	10

I find my partner desirable

1	2	3	4	5	6	7	8	9	10

I am satisfied with our sex life

1	2	3	4	5	6	7	8	9	10

I value my partner

1	2	3	4	5	6	7	8	9	10

I can express my feelings to my partner

| 1 | 2 | 3 | 4 | 5 | 6 | 7 | 8 | 9 | 10 |

I feel listened to by my partner

| 1 | 2 | 3 | 4 | 5 | 6 | 7 | 8 | 9 | 10 |

We are able to discuss issues together

| 1 | 2 | 3 | 4 | 5 | 6 | 7 | 8 | 9 | 10 |

We can resolve issues together

| 1 | 2 | 3 | 4 | 5 | 6 | 7 | 8 | 9 | 10 |

We share a rewarding social life

| 1 | 2 | 3 | 4 | 5 | 6 | 7 | 8 | 9 | 10 |

We share interests together

| 1 | 2 | 3 | 4 | 5 | 6 | 7 | 8 | 9 | 10 |

My partner is verbally abusive towards me

| 1 | 2 | 3 | 4 | 5 | 6 | 7 | 8 | 9 | 10 |

I am verbally abusive towards my partner

| 1 | 2 | 3 | 4 | 5 | 6 | 7 | 8 | 9 | 10 |

My partner is physically abusive or threatening towards me

| 1 | 2 | 3 | 4 | 5 | 6 | 7 | 8 | 9 | 10 |

I am physically abusive or threatening towards my partner

| 1 | 2 | 3 | 4 | 5 | 6 | 7 | 8 | 9 | 10 |

Excess alcohol causes problems in our relationship

| 1 | 2 | 3 | 4 | 5 | 6 | 7 | 8 | 9 | 10 |

I feel criticized by my partner

| 1 | 2 | 3 | 4 | 5 | 6 | 7 | 8 | 9 | 10 |

I am committed to the relationship

| 1 | 2 | 3 | 4 | 5 | 6 | 7 | 8 | 9 | 10 |

I feel secure in our relationship

| 1 | 2 | 3 | 4 | 5 | 6 | 7 | 8 | 9 | 10 |

We have equal responsibilities in our relationship

| 1 | 2 | 3 | 4 | 5 | 6 | 7 | 8 | 9 | 10 |

Overall relationship satisfaction

| 1 | 2 | 3 | 4 | 5 | 6 | 7 | 8 | 9 | 10 |

| 1 | 2 | 3 | 4 | 5 | 6 | 7 | 8 | 9 | 10 |

| 1 | 2 | 3 | 4 | 5 | 6 | 7 | 8 | 9 | 10 |

| 1 | 2 | 3 | 4 | 5 | 6 | 7 | 8 | 9 | 10 |

| 1 | 2 | 3 | 4 | 5 | 6 | 7 | 8 | 9 | 10 |

| 1 | 2 | 3 | 4 | 5 | 6 | 7 | 8 | 9 | 10 |

| 1 | 2 | 3 | 4 | 5 | 6 | 7 | 8 | 9 | 10 |

| 1 | 2 | 3 | 4 | 5 | 6 | 7 | 8 | 9 | 10 |

| 1 | 2 | 3 | 4 | 5 | 6 | 7 | 8 | 9 | 10 |

The Relationship Assessment Questionnaire and all the worksheets and advice contained in this book are offered with the aim of benefiting, improving and achieving positive change in the couple relationship. There will be some exercises that will appeal and work better than others. It will take time and patience together to bring about positive change. It is important to not lose heart if something doesn't work; it will just mean it needs adapting or it just isn't the right exercise for you. There is much to choose from.

In this book, we have covered many examples and techniques to achieve positive change. Chapters have explored special occasions, spending time together, special interests, communication, sexual relations, parenting and meltdowns plus important aspects such as diagnosis and counselling. Keep the notes and worksheets you have both completed in a file and handy, so that you can both periodically revisit them together and monitor your relationship by completing fresh ones and comparing any changes and progress made. Make constant use of the 'pebbles in the bucket' analogy to prevent resentments and unresolved issues from building up, and always abide to the three rules of good arguing. Most important to the relationship is accepting the differences that will exist between you and working with them rather than against them.

Chapter 17

DIFFERENCE CAN WORK

THE discovery of autism offers a couple many choices. If the choice is for both to work at improving the relationship, with or without a therapist, then difference can work. It may take time and sometimes it will feel as if it is all uphill, but with enough love and commitment both can help each other over the rocky bits and when all seems dark. By working together and joining the AS partner's capacity to work out logically how to climb over the rocks with the NT partner's emotional adeptness to help guide them in the darkness, the couple can become strong allies.

I end with two emails sent to me by a couple with whom I performed an assessment. The female partner also attended one of my workshops. They have given permission for their names to be published in this book. The first email is from Mark and the second from his wife Sennur. I believe they portray splendidly just how difference can work, with the right balance between acceptance and understanding of autism, and enough motivation, commitment and, most of all, the love that they share for each other.

> My relationships did not last more than a year, before my partner would leave me, usually for another man… The usual complaint was that I was not affectionate, and unable to talk, and did not understand the difference between sex and love. My response would be that with the next girl I will adjust my behaviour to correct the reason why she left. The problem would be that people are different and what might have worked with the last would not work with the present. I would use drugs and alcohol to deal with my problems.
>
> I fell madly in love with my wife and decided to marry her the night we met. We rushed into marriage and, when my relationship problems started to surface, she took the words until death do us part literally and stayed around. We had our ups and downs, and children, but we always fought over the same things. I lied and eventually started having online affairs and living a secret life. When I was found out we started counselling again to save our marriage. I blamed my wife for making me act the way I did and she was the major problem with our marriage. We spent a

year going to counselling with no success and sessions ending in shouting matches and threats of divorce.

Our incompetent counsellor did not realize that I was incapable of understanding and I was an expert at seeing only what I wanted. The counsellor started to have feelings for me and I was able to make her think my wife was the real problem. When we talked about our sessions it seems that we had a different counsellor and had a different session. In her frustration with me and her determination to try everything to save us, my wife learned about autism and thought I had the symptoms. I did not believe her but I could not turn down a trip to England. I was nervous about meeting Maxine but with the way she tested me and told me I had autism I felt a relief. It was over and I no longer had to hide from others.

Since getting diagnosed it all makes sense now, and I have realized that I was the major problem with our marriage, and I have become better with people.

I'm still semi-detached from everyday emotions and still get wrapped up in the things that I think are important to me – work computers, photography – non-humane things that I can control. But I now realize that I can trust my wife and share things with her. We still have arguments at times and she knows that I don't act the way I am on purpose but it's the way I'm wired. My thought process is still mostly reactive to things – if situation A comes up I'm supposed to do B, but sometimes I should have done C instead, and that's when I get frustrated, when I misread situations. Not as much as before being diagnosed.

The most important thing since being diagnosed is that I can see the hell I have put my wife through and I'm amazed that she is the only one who has stayed around for me. I will try to overcome my inability to process feelings, and try to make her understand that I love her but sometimes it is hard for me to convey it. (Mark A. Simonson)

On the day I was sure my husband [indeed] had autism, I was able to move beyond the anger, depression and negatively infested standstill emotion I had been stuck in for so many years as, now, it had a name: autism. In my thirst for knowledge, I ordered almost all of the books published on the subject. I discovered people and organizations online and, in the process, found Maxine Aston. What a discovery that was. I felt human, I felt validated, for the first time in a very long time, I discovered that the world of autism didn't have to eat us alive. I set a course to make things work for us…

Professionally, I am well versed in various areas, one of which is languages, another is customer service and public relations and, since I wasn't doing a brilliant job as a wife, as I was too emotionally involved, I decided to tackle it as if a consultant to myself. I started banking happy moments with my husband every single day. I made sure we had at least one positive exchange each day and, no matter what he did or said, I did not react. Reducing my reactions to his actions left him without the ability to justify the bad things he was doing. I just kept reading and learning, attending conferences and workshops and implementing solutions in tiny steps. Instead of fighting his addictive personality I encouraged and guided him into photography, created gardens he could sit in and enjoy while he smoked his cigarettes and took pictures.

After confirming what I was doing was correct at a Cassandra Workshop in London with Maxine, I returned to England with my husband and youngest son in tow to meet with Maxine again. Once my husband was diagnosed he actually accepted it and seemed at ease with it. A question he asked Maxine was, 'How do I know how to judge things at times?' To which she responded, 'When in doubt, ask Sennur, she knows.' No one had ever said that to my husband until then and I knew a page in our lives had turned. We had a fantastic trip to England and when we returned home we had a new purpose in our life.

The monster was out of the closet and it was not scary. I was a woman with a mission, with a lot at stake, and it was up to me to set the course. I finally had my husband's commitment to our marriage; he was going to follow and share the responsibilities. At first, we relaxed, basking in the knowledge, letting it sink in, just enjoying each other's company.

We had to learn to communicate more effectively. I learned to ask more specific questions that I knew my husband would respond to more positively and he learned to trust me enough to answer them truthfully. Additionally, I had to learn not to expect!! Such a hard thing for a woman – how could one not have expectations? I simply told my husband what I would like and how I would like it to be done. This kind of clarity helped our relationship. In the end, it was about communication and the style in which we communicated with each other. I understood this well, we spoke different languages and by making an effort to communicate each time, we achieved clearer communication.

If my husband isn't able to do something, he simply says: 'I don't understand this, I am "Aspergic", and could you explain this please?' He explains it's the way he is wired and that he processes things differently. If I tell him what we are doing and when he needs to be out the door, 99 per cent of the time he is there, ready to go, waiting for me in his wrinkled clothes, if I haven't told him what to wear. Then I realize I've forgotten to give him the dress code. We've both learned to leave our egos at the door and stop keeping score. It is no longer about who did what to whom. It is about us and our relationship. Clear and concise communication is in every part of our lives now. We practise it religiously. We do things with goodwill and no longer judge negatively.

My husband appreciates me now; he tells me so, he does things to make my life better and in return I try to make his better too. Autism is woven into the fabric of our lives and we are who we are because of it. We wouldn't have it any other way as we have grown together with it and become better people for it. After 20 years of marriage we are actually looking to the future, to having a lot of great times together. Recently we renewed our vows in Pubol, Spain, in front of the castle Salvador Dali gave his wife Gala. I stood there, listening to my husband tell me how much he loves me, appreciates me and is so grateful for everything I have done to save our marriage. As he held both my hands, gently caressing them, my husband thanked me for being who I am and asked me to never change. All I could say was 'I love you' – I didn't need to utter anything else, he finally knew my heart. (Sennur Fahrali)

References and Further Resources

References

American Psychiatric Association (2013) *Diagnostic and Statistical Manual of Mental Disorders, Fifth Edition*. Arlington, VA: American Psychiatric Association.

Aston, M.C. (2001) *The Other Half of Asperger Syndrome*. London: National Autistic Society.

Aston, M. (2003a) 'Autism through the Ages.' Paper presented to the Families of Adults Affected by Asperger's Syndrome Conference, Boston, Massachusetts, 9–10 May 2003.

Aston, M. (2003b) *Aspergers in Love: Couple Relationships and Family Affairs*. London: Jessica Kingsley Publishers.

Aston, M. (2008) *The Asperger Couples Workbook*. London: Jessica Kingsley Publishers.

Aston, M. (2012) *What Men with Asperger Syndrome Want to Know About Women, Dating and Relationships*. London: Jessica Kingsley Publishers.

Aston, M. (2014) *The Other Half of Asperger Syndrome* (second edition). London: Jessica Kingsley Publishers.

Attwood, T. (1998) *Asperger's Syndrome: A Guide for Parents and Professionals*. London: Jessica Kingsley Publishers.

Attwood, T. (2007) *The Complete Guide to Asperger's Syndrome*. London: Jessica Kingsley Publishers.

Baron-Cohen, S., Leslie, A.M. and Frith, U. (1985) 'Does the autistic child have a "theory of mind"?' *Cognitive Cognition*, 21, 37–46.

Bird, G. and Cook, R. (2013) 'Mixed emotions: the contribution of alexithymia to the emotional symptoms of autism.' *Translational Psychiatry*, 3, 7, e285. Accessed on 09/08/19 at www.researchgate.net/publication/251568591_Mixed_emotions_The_contribution_of_alexithymia_to_the_emotional_symptoms_of_autism.

Bird, G., Silani, G., Brindley, R., White, S., Frith, U. and Singer, T. (2010) 'Empathetic brain responses in insula are modulated by levels of alexithymia but not autism.' *Brain*, May, 133, 5, 1515–1525. Accessed on 09/08/19 at www.ncbi.nlm.nih.gov/pubmed/20371509.

Carter, R. (1998) *Mapping the Mind*. London: Weidenfeld and Nicolson.

Cook, R., Brewer, R., Shah, P. and Bird, G. (2013) 'Alexithymia, not autism, predicts poor recognition of emotional facial expressions.' *Psychological Science*, 24, 723–732. doi: 10.1177/0956797612463582. Accessed on 12/07/19 at www.researchgate.net/publication/236080528_Alexithymia_Not_Autism_Predicts_Poor_Recognition_of_Emotional_Facial_Expressions.

Decety, J. and Jackson, P.L. (2004) 'The functional architecture of human empathy.' *Behavioral and Cognitive Neuroscience*, 3, 2, 71–100. doi: 10.1177/1534582304267187. Accessed on 21/06/19 at www.researchgate.net/publication/51369194_The_Functional_Architecture_of_Human_Empathy.

Fletcher, P.C., Happé, F., Frith, U., Baker, S.C. *et al.* (1995) 'Other minds in the brain: a functional imaging study of "theory of mind".' *Story Comprehension Cognition*, 57, 2, 109–128.

Gaigg, S.B., Cornell, A.S.F. and Bird, G. (2018) 'The psychophysiological mechanisms of alexithymia in autism spectrum disorder.' *Autism*, 22, 227–231.

Gottman, J. and Silver, N. (2000) *The Seven Principles for Making Marriage Work.* London: Orion Books.

Happé, F. and Frith, U. (1995) 'Theory of Mind in Autism.' In E. Schopler and G.B. Mesibov (eds) *Learning and Cognition in Autism.* New York, NY: Plenum Press.

Hill, E., Berthoz, S. and Frith, U. (2004) 'Brief report: cognitive processing of own emotions in individuals with autistic spectrum disorder and in their relatives.' *Journal of Autism and Developmental Disorders*, 34, 2, 229–235.

Holliday Willey, L. and Attwood, T. (2000) *Asperger's Syndrome – Crossing the Bridge.* London: Jessica Kingsley Publishers.

Lawson, W. (2005) *Sex, Sexuality and the Autistic Spectrum.* London: Jessica Kingsley Publishers.

Ozonoff, S., Roger, S.J. and Pennington, B.F. (1991) 'Asperger's syndrome: Evidence of an empirical distinction from high-functioning autism.' *Journal of Child Psychology and Psychiatry*, 32, 1107–1122.

Poquérusse, J., Pastore, L., Dellantonio, S. and Esposito, G. (2018) 'Alexithymia and autism spectrum disorder: a complex relationship.' *Frontiers in Psychology*, 9, 1196. Published online 17 July 2018. Accessed on 22/07/19 at www.frontiersin.org/articles/10.3389/fpsyg.2018.01196/full.

Rodman, K. (2003) *Asperger's Syndrome and Adults…Is Anyone Listening? Essays and Poems by Spouses, Partners and Parents of Adults with Asperger's Syndrome.* London: Jessica Kingsley Publishers.

Salminen, J.K., Saarijärvi, S., Aärelä, E., Toikka, T. and Kauhanen, J. (1999) 'Prevalence of alexithymia and its association with sociodemographic variables in the general population of Finland.' *Journal of Psychosomatic Research*, 46, 1, 75–82.

Shah, P., Hall, R., Catmur, C. and Bird, G. (2016) 'Alexithymia, not autism, is associated with impaired interoception.' *Cortex: A Journal Devoted to the Study of the Nervous System and Behavior*, 81, 215–220.

Thompson, J. (2008) *Emotionally Dumb: An Introduction to Alexithymia.* London: Jessica Kingsley Publishers.

Further reading

Aston, M. (2003) 'Autism in the counselling room.' *Counselling and Psychotherapy Journal*, 14, 5, 10–12.

Aston, M. (2005) 'Growing up in an Asperger family.' *Counselling Children and Young People*, Summer, 6–9.

Aston, M. (2007) *Recognizing AS and its Implications for Therapy.* BACP information sheet G9. Lutterworth: British Association for Counselling and Psychotherapy.

Bentley, K. (2007) *Alone Together: Making an Asperger Marriage Work.* London: Jessica Kingsley Publishers.

Hénault, I. (2006) *Asperger's Syndrome and Sexuality: From Adolescence through Adulthood.* London: Jessica Kingsley Publishers.

Hendrickx, S. (2008) *Love, Sex and Long-Term Relationships.* London: Jessica Kingsley Publishers.

Hendrickx, S. and Newton, K. (2007) *Asperger Syndrome – A Love Story.* London: Jessica Kingsley Publishers.

Holliday Willey, L. (1999) *Pretending to Be Normal.* London: Jessica Kingsley Publishers.

Holliday Willey, L. (2001) *Asperger's Syndrome in the Family.* London: Jessica Kingsley Publishers.

Jackson, L. (2002) *Freaks, Geeks and Asperger's Syndrome.* London: Jessica Kingsley Publishers.

Marshack, K.J. (2009) *Going Over the Edge? Life with a Partner or Spouse with Asperger Syndrome.* Shawnee Mission, KS: APC Autism Publishing.

McCabe, P., McCabe, E. and McCabe, J. (2003) *Living and Loving with Asperger Syndrome.* London: Jessica Kingsley Publishers.

Mendes, E.A. (2015) *Marriage and Lasting Relationships with Asperger's Syndrome (Autism Spectrum Disorder)*. London: Jessica Kingsley Publishers.

Simone, R. (2009) *22 Things a Woman Must Know if She Loves a Man with Asperger's Syndrome*. London: Jessica Kingsley Publishers.

Simone, R. (2010) *Aspergirls: Empowering Females with Asperger Syndrome*. London: Jessica Kingsley Publishers.

Simone, R. (2012) *22 Things a Woman with Asperger Syndrome Wants Her Partner to Know*. London: Jessica Kingsley Publishers.

Slater-Walker, G. and Slater-Walker, C. (2002) *An Asperger Marriage*. London: Jessica Kingsley Publishers.

Slee, K. (2016) *Asperger Marriage and Relationships: Insights from the Front Line*. England: Arc Publishing.

Stanford, A. (2003) *Asperger Syndrome and Long-Term Relationships*. London: Jessica Kingsley Publishers.

Tinsley, M. and Hendrickx, S. (2008) *Asperger Syndrome and Alcohol: Drinking to Cope?* London: Jessica Kingsley Publishers.

Western, L. (2010) *Connecting with Your Asperger Partner: Negotiating the Maze of Intimacy*. London: Jessica Kingsley Publishers.

Further information and research

For more information on Maxine's work and to participate in her current research visit www.maxineaston.co.uk.

Index